# The Fetch

## A Book of Voices

the

Fetch

NICO ROGERS

Brick Books

Library and Archives Canada Cataloguing in Publication

Rogers, Nico
    The Fetch / Nico Rogers.

*Poems.*
ISBN 978-1-894078-82-5

1. Newfoundland and Labrador--Poetry.  I. Title.

PS8635.O427F48 2010     C811'.6     C2010-900661-5

We acknowledge the Canada Council for the Arts, the Government of Canada through the Canada Book Fund, and the Ontario Arts Council for their support of our publishing program.

The cover photograph is courtesy of Alan and Mabel Rogers.

The author photograph was taken by Émilie Fournier, 2008.

The book is set in Bembo and Sabon.

Design and layout by Alan Siu.

Printed and bound by Sunville Printco Inc.

Brick Books
431 Boler Road, Box 20081
London, Ontario  N6K 4G6

www.brickbooks.ca

*for father*

# Contents

# Barking Down a Tree

First, cut into the bark. Use your axe, starting about six feet above the ground, and notch a line down the trunk. Straight line. Soft cut. Not like opening the gut of a fish. Cut only the skin of the tree. After this, cut rings right around the tree at the top and bottom of your line. That done, put your axe aside and work the bark open with your hands. You'll be unsnapping buttons down the backside of a long gown. Work your fingers under the bark, against the wet wood, into the cool, milky sap. In no time, your fingers will be inside the tree, your palms pressed flat against the fragrant wood, fresh as bathed skin. The rest is easy. Slide your hands farther in until your fingertips are touching each other on the back side of the trunk. The rare tree is tant and thick enough that your chest and neck and face will be flat against the sweat of pine, more sweet-smelling than fruit. You'll be holding the tree, feeling hugged against its flesh, within its bark. Now, work your arms down the full height of the cut, six feet or more. The gown peels off. When you step away from the tree, you'll be holding a rind of bark like a cassock of hard skin as tall as you are, maybe taller. Stack the rinds in bundles of ten and pile them all in your punt. With a full load, haul home. They will roof your stores and tilts, your homes, even insulate walls, but they will mostly be used to cover the cod from rain, lengths folded over piles of drying fish and held down by the weight of stones. Stripped, the trees dry up over summer. In late fall, return to your cut lot and take down the standing dead. Haul them home and chop them into splits. All winter, feed your stove.

# Olive Oil

The midwife said you were hardly fit to live a day, coming into the world like that, quiet as morning frost. Nobody in the room, nobody save your mother, expected you to make that first cry. We couldn't help but stare, feeling helpless for you. You were the tiniest thing, hardly the size of Phyllis' hand, with just a patchwork of blue and red and purple lines woven all over that helpless body. And those eyes. Those charcoal black eyes, so full of fear and yet so full of light. A hard type of light. They glowed, dark and bright. And they were fragile, but somehow also like stones. We really didn't know what to think. The silence weighed heavy in the room, and it braced us as we waited for you to shut your eyes. But you wouldn't. So we started to have hope. It took three days for us to understand what your mother must have known all along—her son was born a little red fighter.

We always said Phyllis worked miracles. Every woman around begged for her at every birthing because she ran a tight ship and all the help in the room eased up with her there, knowing there'd be no fussing. We all knew to fall in line, stay steady on our toes, hush up and wait for the word. It was the best we could do. Still, she insists she's not the one who brought you around. When you were just about to become a man, when you'd grown to be twice as big as your mother was, Phyllis told me again she did not save your life. She has saved many, will rarely ever admit to it, but that's not your story. Your mother saved you. "Her soul became his heart," she says. It happened just like Phyllis says, "in the blink of an eye."

You finally came out and Phyllis wrapped you right quick all around with warm damp rags, put you in the stewing pot, and closed the lid. We didn't know what she was up to but we didn't have questions. We just fell in line. She got my sister Rita to put the pot in the warmer of the stove and told her to keep the coals burning as low as she could. She told all of us not to touch the pot, never to open the lid. Right fast, out the door, she chased down Uncle Joe and Skipper Ron to row her to Greenspond in a hurry. When she came back through the door in the middle of that night, we hadn't stopped praying for her safe return and for your mother who was lost in deep unawares and for your feeble little bones.

Phyllis came through the door with a gallon of olive oil and a half yard of new white linen. We pulled you out of the warmer and put that stewing pot on the table. There was myself, Gram, Aunt Neddie, and Aunt Rita all leaned over the pot, each with an ear turned to the lid. We wanted to hear the beat of a small heart, a puff of breath from those tiny nostrils. We needed you to squeeze out a whisper. We listened for nearly a minute. Nothing. We knew we had to keep hope. No one wanted to doubt those eyes, even after you had shut them. Your mother wouldn't let us. She could barely find it in her to speak, she was in such a bad way, having lost so much blood in those hours of birthing, but she didn't have to say a word. Her steady brow said it all. Her boy was going to make it through. She was free of fear.

Phyllis knew what needed to be done. She wrapped the stewing pot in a blanket and got me and Rita to build up the fire in the stove while she soaked the linen with half the gallon of olive oil and told Gram to scrub the bird pan and two bread pans clean as silver. She repeated, "Wash your hands," all the time. "Don't touch it if you haven't washed your hands." She put the soaked linen in the covered bird pan and slipped it into the hot oven, telling us we had the fire too hot and now we had to choke it. She told Gram to scrub down the table with boiling water and set the two bread pans on it. She took the bird pan from the oven, carried it to the table, and opened the lid. A hand of smoke rose to the ceiling.

Phyllis spread the linen over the table using two forks and then reached for the lid of the stewing pot. We all gathered round and she told us to move away. She lifted you out of the pot, uncoiled you from the warm rags, and laid you down in the center of the browned linen. And then she wrapped you up all over again. This time it was done so your face was covered by a flap. Quick as snap, you were back in a bread pan, blanket over top. We waited nearly an hour for the warmer to cool, and when Phyllis thought the heat right, she put you right back into the warmer and closed the lid. She told me to give myself to the fire, make sure it didn't burn up and didn't burn out.

With Rita's help, I kept the coals burning good and steady and low for three long days. No one could open the lid to the warmer except Phyllis. Others spent all their time tending to your mother, trying to keep her soul from bleeding out of her wound. When there was a moment to breathe inside the tense room, we kneeled and prayed at her bedside or in front of the oven where your silent heart lay hidden away. Both bodies either going into death or coming into life, we didn't know which. The black embers in the stove were barely alive too, pulsing red at the core, just the same as your own eyes and your mother's heart.

Every three hours for three days, Phyllis would open the lid to the warmer, take you from the bread pan, and carry you over to your mother's bed where Gram would lower the blanket that covered her chest. Phyllis would lift the linen veil from over your face and take your mouth to your mother's breast. Your red face was not a great deal larger than your mother's swollen nipple. Your two bodies were as silent as the house in which we prayed for your souls.

It was early on the fourth morning, with the sun in crimson over the harbour, that you made your first and lasting call. Softly, a tiny cry echoed inside the warmer. We gathered all around, moving slow, careful not to stir the hope that filled the air. There you were, a constant tender whimper wrapped in warm linen, still hidden away inside the warmer, going on, crying your heart out.

# Praying to Boulders for Berries

All through the end of summer and into the fall, I'd walk the island in search of berries—blueberries and partridgeberries, bakeapples too. I'd fill our Matchless paint cans, sometimes four in one day, and bring them to the store in Sydney Cove. Skipper Malcolm would trade me flour for them. He'd keep a tally of the berries and eventually I'd have a stone of flour to carry home over my shoulder. With that, Mother could bake the Royal Yeast cake that kept us alive. We especially needed it—the cake made from the flour I earned—to get through the long, hungry March month.

If we had flour, we could eat. It was simple. Mother would mix flour and barm that had salt and sometimes molasses in it. Overnight, placed near the wood stove, the dough would rise to the brim of the Royal Yeast can. We couldn't afford yeast anymore but Mother kept the aluminum can from when she had last bought some. She made her own barm, mostly from potato scraps, rice, even spruce needles in a pinch. There were nights I would watch the dough rise, unable to sleep. Early in the morning, an hour or two before the sun rose, Mother would place the blackened can that was once blue and gold inside the oven. Baked, she'd knock the hot heap to the table. I always thought the Royal Yeast cake looked like a new baby: moist, fat, and creamy white. We burned our fingers eating it.

Mother would get six dollars a month for dole. She and three other widows from the island would row to Greenspond. Five miles, each way. Never with the help of a man. At no time can six dollars a month keep a person clear of hunger, especially not a family of four. In those years, it seemed like every house had to set an extra plate at the table for starvation. Only Skipper Malcolm was a penny or two farther from poverty, and it wasn't a penny he kept hidden in his pocket.

One year, 1930, was worse than any other. That was the winter I wore the knees out of my pants, praying so hard. We were in long hungry

March month. We didn't have a crumb to hide from a mouse, and my poor baby sister Addie, Reuben's twin, was too ill to allow any calm to enter our home. I can still hear her cough, a thump in the bottom of her lungs like a knock on rotten wood. She coughed to shake the walls right up until she spat up the blood that Mother was never able to wash out of her dress. A child, cold, collapsed in Mother's arms. For a lot of years after that, Mother only had the blood-stained dress to spare on wash days. She wore a sweater over it, even in summer, but that didn't hide anything.

Maybe it was Addie's death that brought spring on fast that year. I did think, at the time, she had died to feed the long hungry but knew not to ask if such a thing could be true. I counted the days of sun and watched the snow melt. It was warmer and sunnier than any March we'd ever known, but that couldn't feed us. We had gotten hungry enough to make our bones want to surface through skin. Nobody on the island was in a better way. Even the fish dried up from the ocean. None of us knew the whole world was dry at the lips that year. I reminded myself all the time that I wasn't as bad off as my friend Gideon Cartwright. At least my mother hadn't died giving birth to me and, even if Father did drown at sea, at least I wasn't Rufus Cartwright's son. The only thing Rufus loved was the belt and the blood.

I was ten years old and desperate, on my knees as soon as the snow cleared. I had made myself a promise. Before each and every rock in the meadow that was bigger than Addie, I'd drop to my knees, hard and fast, and clamp my hands together in prayer. I'd say "Dear Lord, Jesus Christ, please bring me a berry patch." I'd get up and go to the next boulder and fall down on my knees as if before the altar. Hands pressed to eyes closed tight. I was sealed up inside my words. When I took my hands away under the bright sun, which I knew burned so bright because of Addie, bright reds and yellows poured in through my eyelids. It looked like fire in my mind, and I wanted to see God's face in the flames. I prayed fast and hard to each rock because I knew God wrote his words into stone. I wanted to make a deal with him: Jesus had Addie in his arms and I wanted berries so I could get a stone of flour for Mother and for Dorcas and for gaffer Reuben. I didn't think I was begging. A few berries in the spring of the year seemed so small compared to all our trouble. Hardly a miracle, really. Just a few berries in March, Dear Lord.

I returned home one afternoon with red stains over the knees of my pants. When Mother made me take them off, I was just as shocked as her to see lines of blood running down my shins. I said it was from crushed partridgeberries and blueberries, but we both knew it wasn't. Mother wasn't pleased, cleaning muck and pebbles out of cuts in my mottled kneecaps. I wanted to believe it wasn't blood. It hardly seemed right that a child could bleed from praying. Mother wouldn't look my way that evening, sitting in her rocker by the wood stove, hastily sewing patches from flour sacks over the knees of my pants. She wouldn't look at any of her children. When she finished, she offered me half her cup of tea to drink before making me put my pants on. She insisted I walk across the island to the church in Sydney Cove where I was to beg the Lord for forgiveness for having, as she said, "misused his name and misjudged his nature." She made me swear I wouldn't pray to rocks any longer and wouldn't announce the Lord's name to the dirt.

I went to church and said all the right things. I said, "Good Lord, Jesus Christ, I just want a stone of flour. Mother told me to pray for flour and not for berries so I've come here to you. She's also asked me to ask you to forgive me for having prayed to your name in the rocks." There was so much more I needed to say. I wanted to yell at him. He deserved to hear it. He had forgotten me. He had forgotten all about our island, just as soon as he took Addie. I wanted her back. I wanted Father back. I wanted a great deal more than just a stone of flour for all my trouble and all our pain. I wanted the Lord to hear words that Mother would never forgive me for saying but, in her name, I bit my tongue.

I left the church and made my way back over the hill toward our house in Round Harbour. It struck me then, at the top of the hill, if only for a moment, that Mother must have known how to make the Lord listen. I had done just like she said and, because of it, I smelled fresh cake being baked. The scent and even its warmth washed up the path. I ran home. I hadn't done that in a long time. I was salivating long before I reached the door. I entered with big, hungry eyes, and wanted to cry when Mother told me she hadn't gotten any flour but I had been a good boy. I don't know why I smelled cake. I decided the Lord was cruel, and that, even more than the hunger, made me want to break open. But I wouldn't let myself. I had been pushed too far for tears.

It was dark inside the kitchen. The bit of moonlight coloured the room a tarnished silver. It was a dusty, dead light that paled skin. Mother had Dorcas in her arms, singing soft while Dorcas tried not to whimper herself to sleep. I lay on the floor nearest the oven looking up at the counter with the dirty Royal Yeast can. I pictured the barm foaming over the brim. I wanted to tell Mother she could make our cake now, but I couldn't let myself believe there could be cake without flour. My stomach hurt so much, I could only imagine food. I didn't actually want to eat anymore. I was too hurt for hunger.

We had all fallen asleep in the kitchen. We did this regularly at the time. It's impossible to lie in bed when starving. I was on the floor, Reuben at my side, sharing a blanket. Mother was in her chair with Dorcas across her thighs. We needed to be together in one room or else we'd feel crushed by the emptiness in the house. Middle of the night, we awoke to the creaking of door hinges. Silver dust glistened in all our eyes. Mother's face was nearest the window. She was ghostly. I couldn't look at her face any longer. Hunger was hollowing her. I shut my eyes but the light of the moon wouldn't drown away. Mother's face was in me. I had seen her dead. The wind often pushed the door open, so I thought nothing of it, hoping Mother would shut it or else tell me to. Reuben sat up and rubbed his eyes. He stared at the opened door. There was no wind and no time for me to think a prayer had been answered. Soft, golden light poured into the entrance.

Skipper Malcolm spoke as he stepped in. "Thought I'd bring you this from the store, maid." He had a stone of flour under one arm. "I knows the end of winter is a long and hungry time," he said to Mother. I wanted to jump into his arms but knew better than to come out of my blanket. Mother was not one to accept charity. She would scold me for pitying myself that way, for acting like a lucky beggar. I expected she'd speak abruptly to him, saying she's not the beholden sort. Saying we'd be fine. I was wrong. She said nothing. She looked out the window. She looked down at her sleeping daughter. Vacant eyes. She mumbled something, I don't know what. Skipper shut the door and placed the flour and his lantern on the table.

He stepped towards her. She would not look up. He bent low and rubbed her shoulder. In a low, stern voice I could barely hear, he said, "Don't you be like that. Don't you get down on yourself. You knows damn well you're worth more than that." His back caught the lantern's golden light. Her face was still dusted by the cold moon. "You look up," he said, but she wouldn't. He lifted her chin in his palm. She wouldn't open her eyes. "You always look up, love. This is not your fault. You can be proud." Still, she would not open her eyes, and she would not let her tears fall. Her eyelids quivered with them. I wanted to yell at her and slap her and hold her. I could only stare as she sank inside Skipper's broad shadow, his golden back filling the room. Their breathing frosted the window. Mother hadn't been touched in years. I needed him to kiss her. I needed him to do what Father could do and I couldn't. I needed him to lift her up in his arms and hold her. I wanted to see her arm draped over the shoulder of a man. But he wouldn't and she wouldn't. He turned from her, his hand taking up the lantern. He opened the door to step out but turned toward me with a wink and a half smile. I smiled but it was not easy. It hurt. I regret looking sad because I was grateful. He was gone before I could right my lips. I kept trying to get my mouth to do the right thing even after he'd shut the door. But it wouldn't. I kept trying to right myself but instead broke open. It was a heavy cry. I wanted to drop all of Mother's hard tears too.

# The Drowned

Tossed by a rogue wave, the punt rolls over. Devil's punch. You can't swim. I couldn't either. Doesn't matter. Swimming can't help when the water's this cold. And besides, when your garnsey and long underwear are made of wool and over all that you're in rubber boots and oilskins, swimming don't do much good. You go in, you go down. It's not painless, but it's quick. No point fighting it.

You fight anyway. You go down kicking. The struggle stops before you want it to. Your right arm points up. What is it reaching for? There's nothing to grab. Legs won't kick at all anymore. Face to the sky, there's no beam of light cutting down. No mercy, no God. No hand or eye of the angel. Not even a word for hope down here. The bubbles rise quick: empty balls of air, the last of you. You swallow, choke, burn.

Fire in your lungs so hot it hardens. That's how dying goes in water. Fall, burn, and wait to hit bottom. Hit it and We are found—We are joined. A field of endless fires—The Drowned. We are together. Those swallowed by the dark sea. Welcome. We cannot be seen. We are inside the light and We must burn on.

Call us electric. We are snakes of light that colour the bottom of the sea. We live on inside you, quaking at the heart of the sea, deep inside you. We make you breathe. The air warms us when you breathe. We want you to see that We are The Drowned and We are inside the light, swimming, burning. So speak our names. It warms us and it warms you.

24

# Turning In

Gar turns seventy-two this spring. Today, he split and stacked wood from sun-up to sundown. He enters his home to sit at the table, the sun arching low with evening light. Ruth brings him a bowl of moose stew with the last of the year's turnip stock in it. He eats it fast, starved after a day of hoisting and splitting, but he does so with a plan. He is careful to save the largest cube for last. He does this every year. He is beyond thinking about it. He puts his spoon aside and lifts the bowl to drink the broth. The chunk rests on his upper lip as he slurps the meaty salt juice. He returns the bowl to the table and takes a long look at his last chunk of vegetable. It goes down this way every year—Gar contemplating the end, staring down at the lone yellow cube of turnip.

He never bothers to ask Ruth if she means to cut one chunk as large as an infant's fist. She's never mentioned that she does, saving it, always, for his last bowl. For many years, she's watched him eat and treat the moment as a ritual, a ceremonial send off for the turnip. She still takes pleasure in knowing she plans it so well, but today her eyes are on the budding leaves outside, her face near the window, hands resting in the sink's warm soapy water. The clock clacks. No other sound once her man's slurping stops.

He takes up the chunk in his spoon. It is as wide as his mouth. He mashes it with gums and tongue, his cheeks pressing it back in through the gaps in his teeth. He wants this to happen more slowly than it can. His shoulders arch forward. His eyelids fold over the dulled eyes that drown behind them. He slips inside the memory of an old man who no longer bothers with simple, evening chatter. Savouring his turnip chunk, he runs off into sleep and lands inside a cobblestone corridor leading along stone walls into a fish market. He is floating into the heart of Aveiro, inside a time long gone. Stacks of dried salt cod are loaded in wooden, mule-drawn carts. He sees sealed puncheons packed with fish, *St. John's,*

*Newfoundland* written across each of them. The smell of salt fish washing down his lungs, he breathes deeply, relaxed with knowing well his way around this country of sleep.

He still holds most of the turnip between his cheeks. Puckers up and swallows a bit. It smoothes to cream down his throat and he's off again, this time riding bareback along hills that roll high above the sea, his nostrils flaring to take in a cloud of mare musk. Her eyes are the black hearts of flowers, and he looks into them, resting his bare chest on her head. His ribs thump over her skull. His face is awash in her steam. She is named Flurry. He knows her well. His father worked her in the bush all through his childhood, hauling logs through snow he could get lost in for days. They are riding, thumping along, bodies barely held together.

He collapses into slumber. He breathes deeply, not yet snoring, but that will come soon. His chest expands with each breath. His face floats up. His spirit stretches beyond his aching aged body. He is immense, gentle, a mouth pumping and sucking and kissing without ever doing the world a bit of harm. He pauses. The bowl is empty and the turnip in his mouth is nearly gone now. He loves the pungency. Nothing tastes quite like this ancient vegetable, bitter when raw but sweet if simmered. He inhales, air whistling through dry, pinched nostrils. His lungs expand like gills starved for water. He smells custard. He is sure there is butter passing over his tongue. He digs it into the last of the flesh and nods as if to the taste of thick, sweet cream. Ruth's youthful inner thigh, plump as swollen dough. He smiles.

He swallows. It is nearly over. The mauve and grey patterns of the floral wallpaper blur and fade all around him. An eyebrow lifts as if following the last sweet note of a violin. His lips relax. His nose descends. His jaw slackens. He is ready for bed. His brow droops, and so do his cheeks. The day has been long. The stack of split spruce has reached shoulder height and now spans the house. He can't work like he used to, but he's not done trying. Ruth has started the dishes. Gar can't hear so much as the clink of a plate against the sink, awake or not. He is underwater, drifting farther away. She sees his reflection in the window. She watches his chin bob near his chest. He slouches farther with every breath. Her man is an infant soon to snore in his mother's arms, face smothered in breast. Heart drowned in milk.

# Angel Head

This is a true story. Her name was Roseanne Cheeks, and you'll guess right away where this is going. She'll think you're real funny for laughing at it. We all still call the wife Rosie Cheeks even if she's married to me, Richard Hiscock. She never liked being called Rosie Hiscock. Can't blame her, come too many of the b'ys have taken that a bit far. But forget that foolishness if you can. I wanted to tell you about how I met my Rosie, out by Angel Head.

We'd gone birding in the fall of the year to Popplestone Island, the best bird spot in Bonavista Bay. Sure, if you know the place, you'll think it some distance to row simply for birding, but, as we figured it, by going in a crowd—twelve of us split in three punts and out long before sunrise— we'd make the six mile row worth it. We knew the trip would yield many barrels of salt duck for winter. So, it was at Angel Head Point on Popplestone that I met my Rosie.

Birding was real good, and we had loaded the punts by dinner. Cousin Peter said over four hundred between us, but based on the way he plays cards, I'd have said more like three hundred, maybe a few less. By the time we finished loading the ducks—they were some heavy in the bottom of each punt—the sea was coming on and most of us didn't think hauling home was a smart thing to do. Skipper Reg didn't seem so worried. We were supposed to be comforted knowing he understands the water better than any of us. I say he's never had the sense to hide from her. He says he never gives in to his wife either, but I doubt that part. Peter says he saw her open a can of beans with her bare teeth once.

We all agreed Skipper Reg was in charge because he was the most weathered of our lot. There's no denying Reginald Hunt is a bit of a legend at home. He went adrift bare poles for nine days in the storm of '29 that tossed him and his crew almost all the way to England before they were spotted by a ship that brought the lot of them to port. He returned twenty-one days after having been swept from our end of the earth just in time to join his own memorial service. Everybody saw his wife Dorrie Hunt flatten him on the spot with three punches: first to the chest, second to the throat, and the third with half a kiss to the cheek as she toppled over with him.

But never mind that. It got real dark real fast under all them storm clouds. We were rowing clear of Angel Head Point when someone yelled, "Look, there's a light down the tickle!" We all stared toward Bragg's Island and saw a lantern bobbing in the lop. We squinted our eyes for some time, wondering who would be fool enough to be at sea in a storm of wind like this. The light was coming toward us so we started toward it. Soon, we heard a voice. It was shockingly clear in all that wind. It said, "Hunt! You crazy old fool, you! Never did have the bird's wit to go into harbour, did you!"

We were fast in tow, a row of ducklings following Skipper who followed the lantern into lovely Bragg's Island. We had tea and were warmed to our heart's content by the Cheeks family. Bobby Cheeks was Reg's wartime buddy and the one who led our crowd into harbour. Mister Cheeks said he just knew it had to be his old friend at sea in a "starm'a'wind like that." We were some grateful Bobby understood the ways of Reg. Soon we were into the shine, and Peter took up the button accordion. Ruby, Bobby's wife, said it had sat on a shelf for a shameful long time. Once Peter got to playing, the raging storm had nothing on us.

Oh right, my Rosie. There she was, apple of my eye, hiding behind Mother Ruby most of the night. Mercifully, Peter's fast accordion tunes changed all that. Ruby couldn't hold back once he got to the reels. Bobby said he'd have to replace the floor in the morning if she kept dancing like that. It seemed to spur her on. She must have wanted a new floor real bad because she spun around that kitchen like to bore holes right through the planks. The b'ys were sweating just trying to keep up with Ma Ruby. None of us had ever seen a woman dance like that before. She had feet of fire, up on the table too for a spell. Peter hit all the right buttons, I guess. Meanwhile, I stayed smart. I kept my eye on the prize. I drank my shine real slow and was slipping out the kitchen door with the shy daughter in the corner just as soon as the rain stopped. She and I were never much for dancing.

All right, so it wasn't on Angel Head that I met her at all, but that don't matter none. I like to say Angel Head because that's how I remember it. That's how I like to tell my story.

# Stage

I never really thought you would finally come near me. I mean, I always knew you. I always thought you were the smartest looking boy on the island. Your bedroom window faced mine. When I looked out my window at your glowing room, I could trace your body beyond the linen that kept us from seeing into one another's bedrooms. We grew up like that, curtains between us. I'd gaze at your window and pretend to see inside your dreams. When I did, I made them mine. They were lovely dreams, of course they were—I was in them. I was you dreaming of me, wanting us. There I would be, casting my shadow into the frosted window, peering into the night from my oil-lit chamber, with my little sisters—Anastasia, Verna, and Shirley—teasing me about being forever in love with you, and this is the dream I would dream for you.

You would come walking out of your grandmother's house and descend the path toward the stage. I would be down on the stage, barking nets in the tub, keeping a close eye on that little devil, your brother, knowing damn well he was waiting for his chance to spray water at me—Doffy never did change much. It was a bright summer's day, and you knew I was all joyous because Father and the b'ys had just come home from the Labrador with a great many quintal of fish, and this meant, and you couldn't stop thinking about it, I'd get at least one new dress for school and another for church. You were coming towards me, staring at me as I looked into the water of the tub. You were wondering if I was catching glimpses of my smiling face floating with the bubbles. My eyes were lit with a love you couldn't help but notice. You were thinking about smelling my hair and touching how curly it was in the summer dampness. You felt how happy I was to be wearing my nightgown with little red flowers embroidered into it, even though it was the middle of the day. That's how you knew this was a dream, because mother would never have let me out like that. You loved how I looked like I was floating in a cloud, the sun so lit all over me.

That's when you called out my name and I heard your voice, sounding just like an angel's. You called out to me, nearly singing my name, *Nita... Nita Bride....* I felt something deep inside you stirring at the sight of me. You needed to be so close. I never understood why the dream always fell apart there. I'd have to take over and make it all happen for you. This was when I'd have to force my eyes shut, clamp them tight to keep the truth of what happened from getting inside my head. I was so desperate to keep the dream real, for myself, for both of us.

I would walk down towards me, sometimes with a wildflower in my hand, and I would come closer to myself, and I'd step onto the stage and put my hands around my own waist to hold on to me so tight. I could feel the bones under the cotton of my white gown. With my hands around my rib cage, pressing each finger between the bones, I'd lean over my shoulder and nuzzle through my hair to kiss myself on the back of the neck. I'd smell how sweet I was and enjoy how thick my hair was in the summer dampness. But I couldn't make it last. I'd be forcing myself inside you, inside your dream, struggling to make you real. And then, and this is where I always hated myself, I couldn't control that one part. I'd have to look up from the washtub. I'd have to look at me standing with my face next to my own cheek and I'd have to see it. I'd have to see that you weren't there. You weren't there any longer. It was such a long time ago. We were only children, Sam. I can't stop thinking about you. Oh, my Sam, my Samuel. Why can't we leave each other alone?

# Counting on a Coin

In the spring of '39 I tried everything to get a penny so I could buy an eleven cent can of Old Bugler, cheapest tobacco there was. That's how hard it was for our crowd on Pork Island, not one penny to spare between us. I had found a ten cent piece pressed in the mud along the path to Sydney Cove and believed I was in the fat. I polished it and kept it clean as a secret, buried inside my pocket. I had that coin with me long enough to nearly wear the King's face flat, rubbing it clean every night. As time wore on, it became a bitter fortune because I couldn't buy what I wanted, my first supply of tobacco for cigarettes, a boy's manhood badge. By the end of summer I had learned one thing: you can never foresee how Lady Luck will play her cards.

Old Bugler caused me to get my first real job. I wanted nothing more than to be a man and crack the lid off a can of fresh tobacco, sharp blue as it was with the drawing of a man standing proud on a mountain peak. I wanted to be like Old Bugler himself and sound my horn over the valley below. So, with this in mind, though I was no more than twelve, I lied about my age and went to work on a schooner for a Skipper from Greenspond. I kept the ten cent piece in my pocket the whole time, rubbed it clean in the bunk every night. Three months along the Labrador, on my knees in the hold for more than sixteen hours of the day, spreading salt on layer after layer of gutted fish. Got home with nothing but a slip of paper, an I.O.U. for twenty dollars that could only be spent with the local merchant in Greenspond. The tragedy was, as I quickly learned, Charlie Fitz didn't sell any tobacco.

Mister Fitz took a lengthy time to explain why he wouldn't sell tobacco. Simply put—though that's not how he told it—he used to be a Fitzpatrick. When Patrick, his younger brother, died, Charlie blamed tobacco and stopped selling the stuff. He went on about having to change his family name because it hurt too much to hear his brother's name said in his own whenever someone called out to him or merely said "Morning, Mister Fitzpatrick." Salt in the eye, he said. Twice. "Salt in the eye, b'y." He went on about his brother being too fine of a lad to die before his time and warned me, firmly, shaking his fist and leaning far over the counter, about where I should put my money.

I didn't care for a moment. I had suffered my own loss. In my mind, I was as tough as Old Bugler himself. I had climbed the mountain, stood tall on its peak and was ready to raise my hand to sound the horn that would let the world know I had arrived. Sadly, I was not at all like the soldier drawn on the can—I had nothing to blow into. Nobody was going to smell my cigarette. Nobody was going to notice what I had done with myself that summer. I was peeved, and rightly so. I thought any man carrying Patrick twice in one name isn't fit to live a long life anyway. I didn't say that out loud. Mister Fitz didn't deserve to hear that. He meant well, but, on that day, he meant it for the wrong fella. I walked out, hands in my pockets, and took to kicking rocks along the road.

So, without being able to spend even one penny of my hard-earned pay on a can of tobacco, I gave it all, my whole summer's wages, to Mother when I got home to Round Harbour. She was some proud of me, saying I was as good as the husband she no longer had, the father I never got to know. She could hardly wait to get to Greenspond to restock the larder that had been reduced to little more than bird feed.

In bed that night, I tried to take up the old ritual, rubbing that stupid ten cent piece. All I could see in the glow of the oil lamp was the face of a king I had worked so hard to keep clean, polishing him up like I was a servant picking grime from under toenails. I couldn't take it any longer. It was too unjust. I didn't need the world to be fair but I needed to feel it wasn't hard as rock either. But that's not how it goes. That's just not how life pans out for us low-lots. We never get to break the teeth that bite us. I marched out of the house and launched the snooty face as far as I could into the harbour. I'd had enough of all that foolish hope. Rubbing a coin! Mother put me up to that. And some life she was having. I heard it hit the water but didn't look to know where. I laughed at drowning the king. It made no sense to think that way but I needed some kind of relief. I lay in bed pushing out the laughter, grunting it out, half choking on it, but not letting up until I was sure I had laughed the king all the way to the bottom of the unforgiving sea. It was a sad laughter, but the best I could muster. I felt proud, and I also felt like an idiot. Next morning, I couldn't lift my head. Pain in my side had me riddled into a knot.

The cramp I'd had for the last week could not be ignored any longer. Mother says my face turned the color of dead grass. She has a special way of describing things. She says, "Marbles of sweat were rolling off his forehead," when she tells the story of that morning. It couldn't have been that bad. But I don't pity women when they complain about giving birth. This must have been worse, because I kept passing out and I've never heard of a woman fainting during labour. Mother put two vinegar plants on my chest, which did nothing but smell and make me sweat more than I needed to. Uncle Rex came by to see how my three months on the Labrador had gone. I couldn't speak it out. I wanted to, badly—I had so much to say—but breathing burdened me down so I could barely whisper when I said, "I'll tell you later." It came out in one breath. "Over rum, my son," he said. I managed a smile, but it was smaller than the one I wanted to show. I started to think I was going to have a baby. My whole groin was on fire. I feared I would open up down there. I feared something terrible was going to walk out of me. Maybe I was going to birth out a can of tobacco.

Rex told Mother vinegar plants were for old wives and she should know better than that. He took me up in his arms and carried me to Skipper Malcolm's motorboat, saying to Mother that he'd bring me to Greenspond to see Doctor Weisman. I'd never heard of Doctor Weisman. I started to feel real important. Too bad it was for all the wrong reasons. Mother announced she was coming along, trying her best not to sound excited. I didn't doubt that she was worried, but I knew neither one of us was thinking I would die that day. She tried to comfort me during the boat ride by talking about the food my wages would be good for. She smiled a great deal and that made me proud but didn't distract me nearly enough to clear my head. She went on about the pleasures of salt beef and salt pork. She knew what I liked. She said we'd have a feast, "just as soon as you can stomach it." I listened but thought only of sweet-smelling tobacco and rolling papers. I didn't say a word about my real desires—the idea of smoking a cigarette with my head laying across Mother's lap while she wiped salt marbles off my forehead. "What would you ever wanna smoke for," she'd have said. Hard smack upside the head.

By early afternoon, her and Rex came into the room where I laid. I felt mostly relieved of the worst pain I've ever known. The doctor said I'd faded out not long after he opened me up. I do recall the flash of the knife. It was a special blade, all polished and shiny like it was stolen from a rich man's table. It was a cold, new knife, and I admired it. I wondered where he had gotten it. It was better than a soldier's knife, much sharper than the one I used to clean fish, and that one was real sharp. I know because I used it to trim my nails. I passed out dreaming that Mister Fitz was going to order one for me. He would be happy to. "A surgical blade," he was saying as I faded into the blank, "the choice of a smart young man!" At the sight of Mother and Rex, I sat up quickly and felt seasick. It was as though a heavy metal rod had been pushed through my stomach.

Mother said I looked much better, "face of a clean sky now, my son." Doctor Weisman looked at her smilingly. He must have thought she was elegant, despite having a tear in the shoulder of her dress. She took up my hand and gave me a kiss on the cheek, rubbed more sweat off my forehead. She took to telling me all about the food they had loaded into the motorboat: flour, salt, tea, salt beef, dried apricots and canned raisins, a bag of apples, a can of pineapple juice, and some real tasty dried dates. The list was longer but I stopped listening after she said pineapple juice. What is that like, I wondered. She was still holding my hand when she started about being so proud of me, about me turning into such a fine young man. "Someday you'll tickle nothing but aces out of a woman." I'm not sure what that meant, but her eyes glowed with it. Doctor Weisman announced in the middle of her praise, "Near exploted. Your son could'av blown up!"

His way with words was different than Mother's. I thought she was going to belt him. Had he been a bit younger, she sure would have. Interrupting her like that, in the middle of pouring out her heart. But he was white haired and showed a mouth full of clean teeth when he smiled at her, strangely proud of himself, after he said "blown up!" and tapped his shoe on the wood floor like a soldier reporting for duty. His innocent ways must have got Mother thinking about being polite to him. Maybe she had other ideas. Can't blame her. He was older but had a good straight back, which he liked to display by standing erect whenever he spoke. She always said, "If he's got a back like a good straight plank he won't twist you." He handed Mother a bill with his fee written on it: twenty dollars. My appendix was worth exactly three hard months along the Labrador.

Mother didn't say a word when she saw the cost. She rarely chose silence because she loved her words, but she knew when they amounted to nothing. Her eyes didn't bug out, and her lips didn't clench up. She didn't hesitate or take a deep breath. She didn't have pretty dresses and she didn't have all her teeth and her hair wasn't even combed that day, but she still looked some graceful marching out that door, a real dove, head held high and heels barely touching the floor, Rex fast to follow. Doctor Weisman didn't understand what she was up to, turning around and taking off on him like that. He gave me a worried look, like he thought maybe I'd been left for payment. He hadn't been in Newfoundland very long. I don't know where he was from. I can't even get his accent right.

Mother and Rex were back through the door before I found out where he had come from and how he ever wound up in Greenspond. She stood before him with squared chest and tapped her foot in imitation of him. It was a meant to be a compliment—natural flattery, and a bit of teasing. She was a real flirt. She handed him an I.O.U. for twenty dollars, signed by Mister Charlie Fitz. "Paid in full," she said, ever-proud, smiling just enough to keep her lips from showing all the black gaps in her mouth. No mention of our empty cupboard. She gave him no reason to think that hers were the shoulders of a hungry woman. He smiled at her. She probably thought mostly about touching his teeth. They were pearly. Can't blame her. I wanted to touch his teeth too. He was nice-smelling, good with a knife, and had a funny accent. I've never met another man like him.

We motored home in the evening with a soft breeze over the sea, and a good thing it was calm too because I was laid flat in the cuddy imagining myself to be a tub of beaten guts, bloody and raw and bruised and kicked in all over. My stomach had turned into one big crater in a bloody gum where a tooth had been yanked out by Uncle Mar's rusty pliers—he always threatened to pull a tooth out if you went near his tools. Mother was at my side, rubbing my hand and patting my sweaty forehead with the hem of her dress. I'd had enough. A sense of defeat slipped out of me. "Some luck," I whispered to her, thinking of our endless misfortune. But that wasn't enough. I had to push it further. "Some goddamn luck," I said. I emptied my lungs with those words. I said them hard because I saw the truth. We were a cursed lot whose life was never going to get better. We were bottom-of-the-barrel people, too skinny and poor and ugly to float up with the good fat. She gave me a look of scorn. "Yiess, some luck," she said. "You'd better believe it is. Without your pay, we'd be beholden right now. And that's no way to live, young man. That's no way to live." Her lips tightened for a moment and her eyes burned into mine, shaming me. It didn't last. Mother wasn't one with a need to scorn. She got soft again and started to look like she might whistle my favorite song. Her eyes lit up again, and she gently tapped my cheek and pinched my brow. Her palm was warm on my face. Her touch pushed back the pain. I was still her Ducky and some proud of it. She came into my room that night and handed me something I keep to this day—a shiny copper penny with no trace of a face on it. She pressed it into the palm of my hand and told me what to do with it. "Rub it for good luck," she said, "every night."

# The Man in the Parlour

"Come in. He's in the parlour," she says excitedly, opening the door for you. Now, you are inside her kitchen. She is standing alone near the Waterloo stove, waiting for the kettle to rumble. And then there is nobody in the house with her, not even you. She can barely understand the thought of that—that she is alone, a widow, and has been for most of her life. She spends her time near the window, following the clouds that pattern the sky or losing herself in the crystals that gather and melt over the glass. Only the whistling steam out of the kettle plugs the hole in time.

She does not remember the marriage with a second husband that lasted three times longer than the first. She only remembers the one who got inside her heart. She sits at her table, leaning on her elbows, holding a saucer and the cup that was steaming in the sunlight only a moment ago. Faithfully, she watches the sun rise. She sits in the same place with shoulders hunched at day's end and doesn't see it set behind the house, blackening the hill. She awaits the moon. Her shoulders will lift when it comes, if only a little. Some nights, she stands on her porch to share the night with it. She is always so still, you might think she listens to stars talking across the water.

She enters the parlour as though guiding someone there. "He looks smart, doesn't he," she says pleasantly to no one, gesturing at a coffin laid out along the easterly wall, under the large window. "Come in and see Darius," she says. "He's in the parlour. Go on now, it'll do you some good to see him again." Every day, she reaches over the coffin and raises its lid. With dry eyes, cupping his cheek with her hand, she feels him. He is silent. "You're such a smart looker, Darius. You always were."

Screams of children chasing each other under windows. Disputes and conversations filling the jar of night. She reacts to none of it, never opens the window to the calling of her name. She barely understands that Roslyn, the large woman with auburn hair and an apron whom you saw entering the kitchen yesterday, is the one who usually brings her fresh bread and soup and asks, "How is ya today, Molly?" She always replies, "Come in m' love. He's in the parlour. It's good of you to bring the bread. I'm sure it will do us some good. And soup too! Oh you didn't have to do that, maid." And when it isn't Roslyn, it's either Janie or Flora or you.

Today, staying for tea with your elbows gently settled on the table, your hands rub the hands of poor widow Molly Tiller, cupping them as they quiver. Her words are few and you have heard them often. "So happy you could come, m'love. Wait till ya see how smart he looks in his suit. He's in the parlour." You go in because there are days when you crave the cold fear it takes to make a woman believe in impossible things. Like love that won't ever fade. And you go to be reminded that your own man's casket could just as easily show up inside your home. He too could drown. Any given day, he could. You return to hold her hands and see yourself in her emptied eyes, standing there with Gid and Richard, your brothers, warning you with the same words she heard on that day: "Don't you open the casket, love. He's just not in there. He's gone now, love. Gone for good."

# The Guts

A dog is never more alert, never more in tune with the earth, than when he takes a crap. I look at any dog now as he bends like an accordion to push out the note that brings his bowels into harmony with the grand chorus and I see how it was once the same for myself, a very long time ago. He knows he belongs. His eyes shine with a silent boast that makes me stare with the teary eyes of an envious child.

Used to be I had a sense of the whole damn universe, its grand movement, its cycle of coming and going, its flux. The way the stars are really just sand pebbles along some infinite shoreline. Now I'm old and have only words for how I once belonged to stars and sand, to ocean and rock, the feeling of all that just from going outside, dropping my drawers and becoming simple among the elements of earth. I could sit in that outhouse perched over the sea and reach back to the beginning of time, the ocean groaning below my naked thighs.

My eyes would fill with the clear night sky, the way the dog's eyes do—glistening, focused and empty, opened and ready for infinity. Yes, it used to be like that when I crouched and flexed my belly, back when my cheeks were hard as wooden bowls. I loved watching a steaming turd fall to the wet sand and be washed away in the tide. I was thrilled to witness the power and folly of it all, the ocean and the turd and myself—a trinity of sorts.

I'd send one off like a ship into the adventure of decomposition. I'd watch it float, a rotten star riding night current. I thought of it coming apart with the waves until, by sunrise, it was particles stirring in the water the way dust whirls in the air. That's the cycle. Death floats in water and joins dirt to become blood. I refuse to see the stars as any different. They too are merely hot things that swim along until they go cold and fall apart. I say the ocean is a galaxy, a universe of its own. The ocean universe eats the dust and craps out the life. In that outhouse I saw God. A thing with a monstrous and endless stomach, a galaxy of gases and explosions. One hell of a gut.

In our backyard—it wasn't really a yard; it was more like a country and an ocean too—the outhouse was equipped with a flushing system elaborate as the stomach of God, intricate as the galaxy itself. Between two boulders, at a height of twenty or so feet above the shore, my father laid planks to form the bridge that supported the outhouse. A few minutes before bed, the tide would call out to my bowels the way the moon draws the tide. I'd go barefoot over the wet cool grass and onto the cooler and wetter boulders. The cool and the wet of my feet would light my whole body, electrify me. Like an element of earth, I wanted to grow downward, beneath the surface, to give back to the earth what I had taken from it—this was how the ocean called out and drew me in.

As I skipped over the last boards of the bridge, I'd be undoing buttons and pulling down the trap door of my long underwear. I'd reach for the short cord that was the door handle. Swift as a dog, I'd swing my right leg up onto the floor of the john and, without losing momentum, swing up my left, holding my underwear's trap door between my legs with my left hand. Up and over the height of the bench in the dark, I'd land precisely, arse plunked in the porthole.

When the tide was high, there was a distance no more than the height of a tall man between my perfectly balanced buttocks and the salt water. At low tide, I could stare between my legs at the wet and breathing sand lying flat, a valley between mountains—and I'd sit on my throne, impostor of God, imagining that a train track ran through the valley, over the sand. I'd laugh at the thought of the train having to stop for a steaming mass that blocked the tracks, as if a large pine tree had fallen out of a dark hole in the sky. I'd laugh and watch my pecker jiggle, which doubled my laughter and tripled the jiggling.

There were other times, when I was angry at mankind—like the time in grade school when the teacher, that Miss Rita Pritchett, had a talk with my parents about the family portrait I drew with the crowd of us naked as butcher meat, even the grandparents—at times like this, I imagined the valley was home to a perfect little village. A happy place with boys playing cowboys and Indians, chasing and shooting at each other all day through trees and tall weeds. A place with mothers hanging sheets and clean, knitted socks on the line. Daughters gathering flowers, humming gay melodies about heather and dew and pots of gold. Fathers smoking pipes and strolling alongside their horses and carts through fields, in no rush to cut the golden hay. It pleased me to see them all, especially that Miss Rita Pritchett, get buried under the muck of an inexplicably soft meteorite.

The greatest satisfaction didn't come from playing God, though. I preferred the moments of discovering intimacy within myself. I'd head to the outhouse on a calm night wanting nothing more than to place my whole sensual existence into the cold hands of the sea. At high tide on a clear night, I would walk to the outhouse slowly, feeling submissive, as though in a trance, my arms hanging heavy, my mind orbiting around its own skull. Almost religiously, I went to the high tide like she was the Mother of Mother Mary and I was her lone, loved pilgrim. It was here that I met Oedipus before I ever learned his name. He could have spoken to me in Greek, I would have understood. It was never his mother, not her flesh, that he wanted. He simply wanted to be touched by her wet fingers, to be held by the hands of the source. He wanted to touch and be touched by the womb—and it wasn't about getting off, he would have told me, nothing like that, not with his mother.

I've gone to the sea prepubescent and I go to her in my impotent old age—and nothing has changed. I go to her because we are salt. I remember the first time I tasted my own salt blood, sucking a cut finger.

So sometimes I'd walk slowly to the outhouse, taking my time, letting my whole body be captured and controlled like a sail caught by a gust that fetches it to open sea. The salt spray of waves crashing off the boulders, the water rushing in, convulsing, breathing, heaving over the valley below. Sure it was splendid, sitting on the porthole of the john, looking through the gap in my legs at an ocean like a lung breathing, like a heart beating, like a stomach contracting, rhythmical as a living body. What most made me appreciate the hands of the sea and made me believe that she was my eternal mother was when a sudden wave heaved against the boulders below. A fountain of salt water spraying up through the seat would leave me with no reason to wipe. Few pleasures in my life have been greater than that.

So this is how I've come to appreciate the moment of dying. Whenever it happens, it will happen without my knowing anything about it. It will be like passing through the porthole of the outhouse or being born out of my mother. My end is my beginning. In death, as in birth, we are rushed out of a salt-water belly and dropped into the hands of a stranger. Life's long journey is compressed in that short moment that nobody understands—when we pass from the womb to the washtub to be made presentable and offered up to our mother's arms like a gift, like we are the stranger she has long been waiting for. We get dropped into her hands and immediately take to her fluids. We close our eyes and drink her in. And before we even know it, we are floating away from her to become dust riding the tide.

# Into the Light

I am alone in the icefield. In the distance I see a figure and am drawn to it. It glows whiter than ice—a star lost in daylight. I make the long journey from pan to floating pan. In most dreams, I can leap and fly, but this time every step drags along as if my boots are filled with lead, and I'm terrified of not making it every time I jump over the icy water. It's a hard journey that seems to last all night but, when I make it close enough to the figure of light, I see it's a beautiful woman in a white gown and think good things are bound to happen.

I move towards her and she becomes more beautiful with every step. Her smile and glossy mouth excite me. I am ready to race if she is the prize. She glows like an angel and has a look on her face that sucks the strength out of my knees. I get closer. Her gown is not made of silk the way it seemed to be in the light from a distance. At first, I think young feathers, but soon realize she's draped in the white fluff of pup fur. Her head's inside a furry hood. Its soft hairs tickle her cheeks. She has eyes as blue as the inside of thick ice. Blond hair crosses her neck and flows out of her hood in the breeze. Those lips are red and fat as apples. I get closer. She's inviting me. I swear I'll tear off her fur coat and drop her to the ice if she gives me half a wink.

The dream changes. I should have known it would. It happens like someone outside your head shoves the damper in and the fire gets choked. It's not a race anymore. I can't move so can't resist. But I want to. I am calm now, against my will, but still foaming to be on top of her. She starts to move a little, one shoulder down and the other up, bobbing and batting her eyelashes. She's taking over. That's great. I'll stay here all night and watch. When a woman takes over, great things are bound to happen.

She opens her fur coat and is naked as the day she was born, not even boots on her feet. Her toes alone make my tongue jitter. What a figure, hips and shoulders to melt butter over. She has nipples of bunny nose.

There's not a blemish, not a single bruise anywhere. She doesn't have one day of work marking her frame. And I can hardly believe my eyes. She's got the pot of gold! I've heard that if she's blond at the brow, she's gold in the bush, but I never thought I'd live to see it. I thought I'd have to go to Ireland for that. I'm hard as a fence picket and want to go to it now or die. But it all goes awry.

I should have remembered: women in general but especially women in dreams can't be trusted, not like when you first picture them in your sleep at fifteen years old. You can line them up and fill a yard with them, you're so full of hunger you don't even bother with choosing. You want to die in your bed with a house full of women lying all over the place, each as satisfied and spent as you are, knocked out but still hoping to go another round with you. You can dream a whole night like that and be electric as a storm. When you're young you're full of thunder and lightning and want nothing more than to pound the bedsprings hard enough to break the floorboards of your parents' house. But then something goes wrong and you would prefer to have died. You fall in love, get snipped by love's scissors and pass out from the pain. Next thing you know, you're clamped in a dream with a young naked woman who's there only for a laugh. There's no justice in the world. Especially when women are involved. They find out everything and they justify their accusations without your being aware of having committed any crime. I don't know how they do it, but they always find you out, even if only in a dream. If you live with one woman but dream of another, one of the two is bound to find out. Best keep your pants on.

So, true to form, this dream falls apart. But in a strange, unforeseeable way. A wee seal pops into the woman's arms, out of thin air. She starts cuddling the pup, covering her dinner buns with its head. The pup starts feeding, its kitten mouth locked on her milk tap. I hear the thing moan, the way they do on the ice when you come up to them. With that, a gaff shows up in my hands, again out of thin air, and I get confused so I go limp. I can hardly look at her anymore. I feel ashamed. Ashamed of what?

Looking at her tits? Watching her feed the furry pup? Is that it? You'd think a man would be allowed to run his own dreams once in a while.

So I drop the gaff and raise my two hands as though I've been caught in the act of murder, which is ridiculous, but happens anyway. My hands come up to cover my eyes and I see they're coated, I mean soaked, in bright blood. I can't breathe. I look beyond my hands and there she stands, close enough for me touch. Her white coat is open but has changed into polar bear fur. All down her naked front, right down to her feet, she's got thick blood on her, as if the red has poured out of a gouge in her neck. I look at our feet and then at the ice between us and see there's no blood on it, not a single drop, which makes nar stitch of sense because we are covered in the stuff, smothered with blood. The white pup starts to float between the two of us, and it's clean as the snow, hanging in the air like it's been the angel in the dream all along. It moves above us, and now all I see is her. We stand face to face.

Again she changes. Now she has more makeup pasted on than is sensible for any woman, no matter what her face looks like naturally. It's a mess, and it worsens as I watch. The makeup spreads out of her eyes and nostrils. It ends with black splattered around her eyes and running over her cheeks like she's been punched with it. There's blue over her nostrils and it's bright. She's been turned into a beauty ad left out in the rain and trampled on by a team of horses hauling a wagon. Horrid! Her lips are smudged with bright red wax and it covers her busted cheeks and chin. She's a wreck of a woman. Imagine, a figure I thought was an angel, someone made of light from above, now about as attractive as a festering wound.

Not the dream I had hoped for. I just wanted her to take off the coat. It could have ended there. I don't get why moving toward the light had to turn into such a twisted journey. I feared I'd die trying to get across the ice, trying to make it to the light, which I didn't know would turn into a woman. When she opened her coat and showed me a naked body, I was sure the gates of paradise were next to spread and St. Peter would be there to spur me on, telling me I'd been a good man and deserved every sweet thing death had to offer. So why did it go like this? Why would she turn horrid-looking?

There's no point to it. In the end, she just went her way. Disappeared into thin air. There was only myself and the pup. Which didn't float anymore. It was normal again. We were both on the ice in a world that was white and pure and frozen. I liked how I felt innocent again, even with the gaff in my hand and the pup at my foot. I guess a woman like that just isn't meant for the ice. She's made for a young man's dreams. There's nothing real to a woman like that. I say she belongs in a jewelry shop. That's all she's good for. Besides, she couldn't handle a man like me. I'd a been up and down her backside making her scream about thunder and lightning and wanting to die with me, again and again, right there on the ice.

# Touched

Uncle Hump's rightful name is Henry. He is arched over so steep these days he hardly bends his knees to enter the root cellar. It's always been a queer thing to watch, him and the cat. When the weather shifts and the clouds show they don't really know what to do with themselves, he gets some awful pain in his neck and shoulders. His grimaced face—a toothless, tobacco-blackened mouth—tells only the surface of how he feels, deep inside, at bone-level. The only cure, he says, is to keep his cat Tilt balanced on his hump. He walks around most of the day like that, in the garden pulling weeds or at the wharf barking nets with the children and women. He splits and stacks junks too. All the while the cat rides his hump, righteous as a princess perched on a camel. She's gotten old and feeble, though, like him, so she latches on for the ride.

The story of the cat goes like this. She jumps the wharf in S'n John's to board the Ruby Plowman, some twenty years ago, not knowing she's just set sail for a place without alleys or fish markets and with no butcher or tavern scraps in the gutters. There are no gutters. She's bound for an island marked by six simple homes, no big buildings, no cars, and no cats. But, as fortune would have it, plenty of mice arrived the same as her—freeloaders aboard the Ruby Plowman. On deck at sea, not more than an hour beyond Signal Hill, Hump hears a muffled meow coming from under a turned-over skiff. He kneels and sees a kitten strangling herself in a web of fish net. She is frantic when Hump's big hand pulls her into the open where he untangles her limbs with a pocket knife, nearly slicing into a white paw to set her free. He calls her Smurr on the spot, and I don't know why.

Ma Moo, christened Hamutal but called Ma Moo or Moo but never Mute or Ham, as some Hamutals have been, was cook on board the Ruby Plowman. She took to the kitten the instant Hump came down from the deck holding her, dumbfounded. She kept her in the galley for the long three days it took to sail home in unfavourable winds, feeding her all the salt pork scraps she'd eat, pouring her saucers of tea, too. Smurr found a strange love for hot tea. And would she get perked! All wired in the eyes just like the light bulbs Hump and Moo never lived to see over a table in their home. But the good life didn't last long. The kitten took ill.

Smurr looked like the forest floor in fall. Her coat of red and gold was churned like leaves in a heap of pine cones, lichen and dulling daisy petals, with a few strokes of devil's paintbrush flaring up through the heart. Sharp, clean snow patches on all paws, tail and underbelly. She looked like chaos in a nutshell but she still had a stare for the world with eyes the blue of a calm sea. It could have all been a trick though, as beauty often is. Could it be the dying that made her so fetching? Her infected ear frothed pus and her blinking slowed while the Ruby Plowman faced a howling headwind, her crew tacking hard in their fight for home.

When she landed in Round Harbour, Smurr might as well have been covered in ice. She was shivering down to the claws. In that last day at sea, she had declined so much that just to stand on her legs made her shake as if she were at cliff's edge in a gale. Her eyes were dulled to the grey of a cloudy day. Inside their tiny and tidy home, Ma Moo told Hump what was needed. He fetched it all in a hurry, and by the time the kettle was rumbling Hump was at Ma Moo's side, carrying a Matchless paint can filled with three handfuls of spruce needles and five strips of sappy bark, a fist of yellow lichen, leaves from a blueberry bush, and twenty or more tiny purple flowers, the delicate ones that only grow inside the cemetery where it's open to the sun.

Ma Moo packed the pot with the ingredients and then drowned them all under steaming water. Boiled down to sludge, she strained the mixture through cheesecloth, then added lard, molasses, vinegar, and "cure-all": kerosene. Mixing a poultice, Moo never doubted her senses. "Lassie and karseen," she said to Hump, "that'll bring kitty up again." Hump nodded. He believed in Moo. He held the kitten in his lap and rocked her by the window. For four days, he rubbed glistening sludge into the cat's ear. The house smelled of sweet and bitter cure-all. He even served her saucers of tea. But all the care amounted to nothing, or so it seemed. It looked like she was fixed on dying right up until the middle of the fourth night.

Hump was deeply asleep in the rocker, shoulders hunched over the kitten, when her eyes suddenly opened. The clouds had lifted. Her ears pointed up. High alert. Alive again but without memory. "Who is this man," she must have wondered in the middle of her stretch, back arched up to his nose, before she panicked and locked all her claws into his lap, puncturing pants, then skin. Too much tea and sleep? Had the lassie and karseen soaked into her brain and driven her temporarily mad? Either way, in that moment she was hell-bent on showing Hump she was no sissy puss. Hump leaped from the rocker, yelling as if the devil had just dug his heart out with a rusty spoon. He cursed and launched the cat across the room. His memory was not operating either. Ma Moo rushed into the room and quickly retrieved the cat from under the table. "Oh, she's terrified of us now," she cried, working to smooth the raised hackles. Smurr was slow to drop her guard, but eventually she calmed down and snuggled into Ma's shoulder. Hump settled back into his rocker, rubbing his gouged thighs, readying himself for one more night out of his own bed.

Sometimes Ma Moo still calls the cat Smurr, but Tilt is the name the animal turns her tilted head towards, rarely choosing to walk towards the voice that calls her. Lopsided, the cat walks on. "If they calls me Old Hump," Hump said to his cured cat one day after they had made up, "I'm gonna call you Tilt." As though to acknowledge she was grateful to be healed, she eventually taught him something too. On a dozy afternoon, she climbed Hump's shoulder while he was napping, slouched in his rocker. She snuggled into a ball over the hump between his shoulders, one white paw resting on the back of his head, purring away like a tiny outboard engine. Hump snored deeper, slouching further forward with every breath. He always slouched in his naps, but now he was folded right over, arms almost touching the floor. Tilt purred on, her warmth penetrating down to bone level. She was repaying the work of Hump's steady thumb on her infected ear. The pressure of her rumbling body had relieved him of a pain that not even Ma Moo's best liniment could clear away. He awoke, rested like never before. From that day on, they were inseparable. They were one body, half human, half feline.

# Bottled Up

I'm up before the sun. I don't leave much to chance. I don't trust anything. There's no way to know what the day will do. Life's hard, made for work and death, and if you don't work you die. Straight and simple. Idle men are dying men. Look at me. I never put my hands in my pockets. I'm always ready to work with my two hands quick as my eyes. I'll throw you overboard if you stand around with your hands in your pockets. I didn't become skipper of my own schooner at the age of thirty-six from some God-given right, and I never inherited one privilege from a drunken father who died the same way he lived, as a heap of shit. He fell out of his chair and hit the floor. It was morning. I found him at midday and stared at him for a minute, without blinking. I told him he could be proud of getting one thing right, and then dragged him outside and got the mop to clean up the mess.

It's not easy to call things what they are, but I'm a man of my word. If I say it, I do it. No one questions that. If I let up and give in, I know I'll turn into him and spill over dead, like a barrel of guts not worth the time it takes to mop me up. I know he's in me. I know how it works. I keep an empty bottle of rum on a shelf to remind me. I keep a long thin straight razor beside it. When I look at the bottle, I see his boozing. I stare at my warped face in the bottle, knowing damn well my father's fetch moves inside it. Listen to the blade scrape the stubble under my jawbone. I smile and sometimes draw blood, holding the curse by the neck.

I bought the bottle not long after they buried him in the hole I refused to help dig. I stood on the pier in the dark before sunrise and swore two things: I would not drop a tear, and I would never take a drink. With that, I poured the rum into the sea and kept the bottle to go with the blade. I keep them both, bottle and razor, to remind me of that morning, of what I swore to, and of my old man who wasn't worth the weight of his bones. If I turn to the booze, I turn to the blade. If I swallow, I slice. Straight and simple. If I say it, I do it. Mark my words.

# Sweet Vengeance

Tom Cane points to a lone pup across the pan and says, "You can have that one, my son." I was excited by the offer. Thrilled and touched. It was generous of him. To look at the man, big and brutish, you'd never think he'd offer anything, let alone an easy-to-fetch pelt. But Cane has a reputation, so I should have seen it coming. He must have known, just to look at me, a mere pup myself, that I was blind to devilment. Green as a June hillside.

This one seal hadn't been killed. Strange, I thought. We'd been at work around it all day and I'd never noticed it. Nobody had noticed it? We'd covered the entire icefield, killing hundreds, and there were countless boot prints in the snow surrounding this lone pup. I do remember thinking, as I walked toward it, that maybe if a man is enormous like Tom Cane—he was about three times my size, and I'm not the smallest sort—then maybe he has a bigger heart than other men and that must make him the giving sort.

Following footprints that led nearly to the pup's nose, I noticed someone had walked right out to the thing. And didn't club it? Why didn't a light go on in my head? So I was following these footprints when—like the drop of a mallet—I fell through the ice. I don't swim. I didn't think about that. The water was colder than ice, as you can imagine, so I wasn't about to start making sense of things like how do you swim if you can't swim. I skipped the trying to swim part and went straight to squealing and howling and yelling.

Everybody else had been to the ice with Tom Cane so they all knew about his trap. I'm sure most of them lost the green behind their ears down that same kind of icy hole. When I got out, Tom was proud to show me the pair of boots tied to two long arched sticks that he used to press footprints into the snow just covering the hole. You can imagine all the mad laughter for yourself. There was lots of it. Anyway, there I am drowning in the coldest water possible, and the others are laughing their guts out. Somehow I got hold of the ice edge and a couple of boys grabbed me by the collar and yanked me out. It felt like I'd been dropped into a huge mouth full of needles.

I didn't want to come across as being too clever—that creates its own set of problems—but I needed to let Big Cane know I wasn't gonna be his roll-over. That Saturday night I knew he'd be on the shine. I tied a trip string from a can filled with molasses that I'd fixed to the planks above his bunk.

Picture it: He's stumbling between the bunks. His shoulders are as broad as a hallway, and the stacked bunks are all that's keeping him from toppling over. He's been a swiler so long that he has his own bed, an extra large one that takes up a corner. His drunken walk is well rehearsed. He reaches the bunk and falls into it with all the grace of a tossed carcass. His head hits the string but he's snoring before his eyes are shut. Out cold. The lassie pours over his eyes and nostrils and lips. It's in his beard and leaking toward his ears, but he pays it no mind, just snores on. No word of a lie, there were black bubbles blowing out his nostrils and popping over his lips. Tom Cane, dumb drunk on shine, ready to sleep the whole night through. No witness on board but me. The rest are all asleep. I nearly piss myself.

So, next morning, the crew is awake bright and early for Sunday morning prayers. Someone notices Cane and calls us all to gather round. There we are, with our heads over top and in between and under each others' bodies. The lot of us looking at the big lump snoring with a face like a black bear's. His big mouth is wide open. His tongue is like a little red capelin trying to swim its way out. When he starts to stir, the whole crowd rumbles, split open by laughter. All this lasts a good while. He stirs more and starts to jerk about until he lets out a snort. Then he snorts again. He's in a dream we all understand—he's a bull moose at a cow in heat. He raises his hand up to his face and rubs from his forehead to his chin. He pushes the molasses all through his beard and then up again, over the hair of his head. He doesn't wake up. He's gone right back to his dream. And snorting more, faster and deeper. He must be close to that cow in heat, his nostrils flaring. He puts his hand down his trousers and starts to perform the morning ritual that most of us will seek privacy for, if ever we can find it—the privacy, I mean. Pretty soon, he's all snort.

We have become a bag of mixed birds being tossed around, squawking, screeching, chirping, screaming, and howling in every imaginable pitch. Laughing like to die. And then he wakes. To silence. Tom Cane is a monster. His eyes, so white in his black face, are staring right at us, and then at me. He sees I'm the one who's thinking about running. I piss myself with fear. We all know he could take any six of us in his fury. His tongue has a taste of what's on his lips. He gets it now. He doesn't think it's funny. He sits up fast, ready to charge, cracks his head into the planks above and knocks himself out. He's lying back in the bunk, blood mixing with the lassie on his forehead. He's breathing, though, so nobody goes near. He takes to snoring with his face contorted by rage, one hand still pinned inside his pants.

When he came to, we were all on deck, standing in rows under the open sky for Sunday morning service. Not one of the boys had room for the Lord's name in their mouths—none but me. I never prayed so hard in my life. I didn't have to look around to know what the other men's faces looked like. I knew each of them was grinning from ear to ear, imagining Tom Cane pulling his hand out from of his pants, raising it over his face to rub lassie into the lump and cut on his forehead. "What the hell?" tumbling out of his mouth. No more the bull moose snorting for his cow in heat.

# The Deep

When the water is calm, I can follow the rock bed of this island. I can see how it reaches under the water. How deep it goes, I have never known. I know nobody who does. Inside the harbour, that's one thing. At the end of the wharf, you can see bottom, with tansies and scullies moving under and around the rocks—the odd oil can too. But along the shore that faces the straight of Long Hungry nobody could ever build a wharf. It's that deep.

The moon is one thing. Mysterious, yes, and meaningful. Easy to reach with the eye. And sure I know I'm supposed to wonder about the stars and the creatures they form. But I have no questions about stars. I just want to know: how deep is Long Hungry?

# Tail

If you had any strength at all you'd have your heart in your hand the way your father did and the way your older brother does, but you're a shaky one, always lured by the boulders, by the voices of sirens hidden inside the crags of shorelines, drawing you magnetically. If you had any strength at all, you'd stay in the common, anchored at the center of the harbour, knowing full well that storms give little warning and leave only the fallen as proof of their rage. But you love exposure. You can't help it. You've had mermaids in your mind ever since hearing they were bare breasted, fabulous as hospitable angels, generous to their tattooed core. If you could just understand that the world has a great deal more to offer than the draw of a woman's bare skin and the crevice of flesh that swallows your every dreaming minute, then you'd finally get it. You would forever believe that human satisfaction—the full pot of existence—is little more than belonging, and that belonging goes hand in hand with keeping your mind within the four loving walls of your house, your home, your family.

But it can never be that simple for you, can it, never that genuine, that wholesome, that good. If it's not dirt, it's dirty, and no matter how hard you scrub out your skull, you can't seem to get your head clean. You just keep on wanting, devouring memories of brushing your hand against female cloth while dancing to Gideon's wild accordion in the late night of a sheltered Labrador harbour, or inside those nights in St. John's at the end of a lonesome summer's toil when you'd stumble drunkenly off a brothel step and fall face down in the dirt, your pants hardly pulled up and your pockets emptied of hard-earned pay. It's not that you don't love your wife, lovely as a spring flower. You're just not strong enough to believe in perfection, to anchor your boat in the heavenly real, the harbour of home. You can't forget how you felt inside your body when you first desired the wanton flesh of the stranger, the bare-breasted mermaid, tattooed in flames from shoulder to wrist, the same fiery story curled in her seaweed hair and singed all down her back—the handprints of a thousand burning sailors. The endless dream of the longed-for lady of the sea who visits you faithfully while you float lonely past strange shorelines, watching for her swerve beneath your punt, scanning the dark sea with nostrils flaring, blowing steam into the frigid air, dreaming away inside the blanket of fog, calculating how to ensnare her body and blindly believing that emptiness of soul need not always follow the body's longed-for release, that you will not again hear the hum of your exhausted heart, leaving you wanting more, with the desperate belief that to master the secret of the senses, to discover the key to the forbidden world of the body, to solve the mystery of the mermaid's tail, is finally to achieve the impossible.

# Rosebloom

You've got to get right in there. Hook your finger around the back of its little head, give it a nudge with the crook of your finger. You've got to tell it to come towards you, coax it into life. You might feel like you're trying to sell it something it doesn't need, but that's just part of it. No matter what, you can't give up. You've got to talk to it with your finger, let it know it's not going to be alone in the world. You say, "Come here, little goat, time to get out of there. Leave your poor mother alone." It's queer how it works, really. Being born. The most awkward thing we do in our lives. For goats or people, there's not much difference. It's as if we all have a need to hide from the beginning. We come into the world knowing we don't want to die.

Rosebud was some big that year. By the time she was ready to break open, she was wobbling about lopsided, a boat with its ballast hove to one side. It took the poor creature some terrible time pushing the first little carcass out of her. I was trying to hook the back of its head with my finger, but all I was finding was a hoof where the head should be. In the end, I had to pull that one out dead and drop it in the hay to be burnt. The next one was white as an angel and didn't live long after her first drink from the teat. Some terrible mystery to that one. She was a solid little creature that looked as strong as Rosebud herself. But she didn't live more than one hour. Never even got the chance to name her. That made two dead in the hay.

The third one is what broke our hearts. Rosebud's too. It made me afraid that she would never give life again, that her body would lock up and she'd become a sad old maid when she should still be ripe with youth. This little buck was black as night across the face and over the arse end, and everywhere in between he was a quiltwork of brown and white—queerest looking creature, but cute enough to crack a glass eye. We called him Swirly, partly because of his senseless mess of hair patches, but mainly because of his deformity. In the middle of his back, his spine made a sharp curve, like a root would to get around a stone.

Within minutes of being brought into life, he was milking at Rosebud's swollen teats and she had finished licking him clean. After his feed, up he went to find his feet. He found the front ones, then tumbled over. Up he tried again. It seemed his hind end believed it was still inside his mother's harbour, not just yet willing to go to sea. Rosebud got up on all fours and left the tilt, eyes to the ground, interested only in the grass along the fence. Swirly called out to her. Rosebud wouldn't look back.

Esther and I couldn't leave the little buck like that, not when we saw him trying so hard. She picked him up, all four pounds of him, and brought him inside the house. We needed to keep him warm. I got Rosebud in collar and brought her into the house too, tied her to the Waterloo so she could wander only so far from her unwanted son. And then we coaxed her. At first she'd have nothing to do with him. We'd put his pink little nose to her teat and she'd crack her hind leg, jar his nose away. She just wouldn't allow it. So I held her hooves to the floor and Esther got Swirly's lips into the fat of his mother's milk. We fed him a full day like this. He seemed to be coming along. Strong in the eyes, wet on the nose. He never found his hind legs though. Just kept falling over. By nightfall, his eyes were dimming.

Esther touched my shoulder and went to bed. I wasn't gonna give up, knowing the way I came into the world, terrified of living. They say I came quiet as morning frost, and that was Swirly. I was kept in a warmer in the stove. Imagine that. I took four days to cry the cry a baby makes when it decides to give up on dying. I had to give wee Swirly one more night, one good chance at life. I worked an old baby bottle full of Rosebud's milk and, so long as the moon was witness, I kept coaxing crooked little Swirly to drink. But, little by little, the life dropped out of his eyes. He could barely breathe. I put my hand over his mouth and nostrils and hugged him hard. Come morning, I laid his carcass in the hay with his sisters and tried not to think about burning flesh while I stared into the sunrise, wondering too much about life.

All summer, Rosebud wouldn't go near any of the young goats on the island. If any came near her, she'd steer clear. Never push one or bully it, just lug away. But one of them caught her somehow. When we saw she was pregnant again, Esther and I rejoiced but not without fearing the worst could happen again. On the morning I found Rosebud laying in the straw, hidden away in the corner of the tilt, I knew I needed to stay close by. Come midday, she was breathing heavy and fast and had gotten up on all fours. I could see by the valleys formed at either side of her spine that the young had dropped low and were ready to come out. I got in behind and saw that her passage was swollen. Before I was ready for it, a little black hoof was pointing out of her. Again! I got my finger in there to find the other hoof and pulled it forward, so both hooves were side by side. Then I waited.

Poor Rosebud was breathing hard and pushing the best she could. No sign of the kid's nose, no reason to believe that this one was going to come out any better than the last three. So I got my finger well in there and felt around for its face. Found it. It was twisted to the left, so far back I feared for its neck. But I wasn't gonna give up. You can never give up. Softly, I worked its head towards me with my finger and lined it up so that the little pink nose was in the air, resting on the two hooves. Rosebud pushed some hard. That wee face peered out of its mother, almost to the eyes. And then the pushing stopped. I feared she was dead weight.

I didn't fret much. I simply worked my finger in behind the head and softly nudged it toward me. It wouldn't come out. I knew I couldn't coax too hard, fearing the neck was already close to broken. Then I tried something I never did before. I got my finger in behind the top of the head and circled down the face and neck and under the hooves, then back up along the other side of the head. By the time I got back to where I had started, all the pressure Rosebud had built up inside burst through and her kid was launched right out into my lap. Knocked me over.

Poor Rosebud dropped to the straw, hind legs quivering, covered in black fluid and blood. I scrubbed the little one with handfuls of straw, and the three of us lay down in the hay, exhausted. That kid weighed enough for two, almost three. She was twelve pounds, the biggest-ever. Once she got up and took to the world, poor Rosebud could hardly eat enough grass in the weeks to come. She was feasting and starving at once, eating to feed the kid who was sucking the milk out of her faster than she could make it.

# A Clean Beating

It happened all at once in a ritual nobody talked about. Each thump of the swinging brooms struck the cliff and came back to us as we busied about our Saturday morning chatter or listened to Pappy whistle old jigs and reels.

The beating didn't last long, but surrounded us like fast drumming in no particular rhythm, like hail falling on rooftops. It was needed, the beating. We children understood that much.

I can still see all the women on their porches, hands locked on broom handles, eyes squinting, arms swinging and striking. In their silence is a tremendous satisfaction as they raise a whirling cloud of dust.

All these years later, I can hear it still, the whacking, thumping reminder of how good it feels to beat your mats perfectly clean.

# Best Hand Ever

I was grateful when I got my hand inside her skirt. She was not convinced. She needed to know I was a man, not a boy getting lucky, dealt the wild card after betting a bluff. There was no bluff. Both of us knew we weren't in the game for love, not at first. There were no lies between us. I played like the joker, but *she* was the wild card.

It started with her brushing up against my shoulder with a breast that outweighed my arm. At church and on the wharf and in the post office, current stirred in our eyes. When we collided on cemetery hill that night, wildflowers were making their way out of the dirt. We lay in cold spring grass, the smell of her neck too sweet for the rough ground. But in her mouth, in our mouths, breath was lively as fresh moss. I pressed my hands over her breasts while the moon glistened in her black hair. I watched her breathe. Her eyes closed. The frost of the cooling night, shimmering in the moonlit air, entombed us: we were sparkles in black marble.

I moved my hand up her woollen legging, slowing to circle her kneecap, before pushing on with my palm against her thigh. When my fingers pressed against her passage, the scent and feel of lips opening made my eyes roll back. And that's when she shut down the game. "No more," she said, "not without a promise." I had to fold on the spot. I had been played. I didn't bother with the big question, I simply said, "Yes, love." She said, "See the preacher in the morning." I did. Bright and early, before he'd even thought of saying his morning prayer. I was back in the game then, with a fresh deck. Now we were partners: Joker and Wild Card. Wed as the wildflowers were reaching full bloom.

# Fatty Me Mommy

I look Fatty into the eyes and I looked into her eyes because they were big ones and I can see my head in there and I am round headed like a ball and I like to see my head round like that because it's funny and since Mommy went into the sky I live in that house here but Huncle is a grumbler and doesn't talk to me very good and has a tight face on his skin and all I do to Aunty is make her lips get hard and she has two big yellow toofs in her mouth that stinks and when she looks at me with her mouth when she yells at me she wants to bite me with her two yellow toofs and I wish the boy Lucence could be good but he bangs the rabbits and pulls their ears in his hands and makes them go round real fast and sometimes lets go but rabbits don't fly so there can be blood on the rocks and once on my dress on Sunday because the boy Lucence hit me on the back with the rabbits and Aunty smacked me in the face because the blood is on my dress but no one wants to listen because Aunty says my daddy was the devil but I don't know that and that's why I always talk to Fatty because I can't let myself be nice to the boy Lucence but Fatty has bigger legs than me and I can touch the funny snakes inside there when I can push on the snake to make it go empty and when I let go of my finger the snake fills up again with the white blood but blood is red so Fatty has milk in her legs and that's why she's so fat cause she has lots of milk in her bellybag and that's where I like to put my hands because they can get cold and her bellybag is hot and has skin like my belly but I don't have funny fingers on my bellybag so that's why when Huncle is gone away on the water I can get under her bellybag and play with her fingers and sometimes I can get thirsty under her and Fatty is happy when I look her in the eyes and play with her funny fingers that's how come I know she doesn't bite me when she kisses because I used to think her yellow toofs could be like Aunty's toofs and that's how come she kisses me with her nose so I'm not afraid but that makes my face stink and I don't want to like my stinky face but I like Fatty so Aunty can hit me if she needs to make my face not stink like her face stinks when Fatty lifts her tail and I can make stinkies too but not good like Fatty because I don't have a tail and my stinkies aren't green not yet but one day I want a tail like Fatty so I can have a little sister pull it and she can look me in the eye and see her face in me and if the boy Lucence comes yelling holding his rabbits by the ears she can hide behind me because Fatty doesn't like the boy Lucence and his rabbits and one time he put his gun to Fatty's eye but she didn't look at him and I was crying and he yelled a mean Bang but Fatty is bigger than the rabbits so the boy Lucence had to push me into the dirt but Fatty looked at me and said it's ok because the boy Lucence is smaller than she is and big people don't understand that much so that's how come I really don't like to watch when Huncle hits her bellybag because his hands are mean and sometimes they hit me but Fatty can moo and lift her tail and make a stinky when she doesn't like Huncle to pull her fingers and to yell at her because she's not stupid and nobody listens to Fatty and when Huncle and the boy Lucence couldn't bring her to the wharf today because they pulled at her head and hit her with the wood on the big bum and told her she was stupid I had to go see her when Huncle pulled me by the arm and made me walk her to the wharf where I tried to kiss her and tell her everybody is smaller than she is and then I could only see she in the eyes when Aunty put me in her arms near her toofs and the boy Lucence yelled a big Bang Bang with his gun at Fatty again and laughed at me and Fatty and now Aunty put me in my room under the stairs and told me to stay here or she can hit me real bad so now I have Grumpy in my arms but he can't talk like Fatty and I know Fatty wanted to kiss me with her nose and so I kiss Grumpy because he's a nice bear and Mommy made him with Daddy's clothes and I like Mommy's pillow and that's why I want to go see Fatty because I miss Mommy and I want Mommy to see Fatty so she can tell her where the sky is and that way Fatty can take me to Mommy because Mommy's not here and now I miss Fatty and I want Mommy

# Lucky Boy

The game was called copy and the point was to keep from falling into the water—you had to be some smart to save the pan from tipping over, keep yourself from sliding under. It was called tippy too, but only by the young ones. When you became boy enough to know that this wasn't merely a game but training for the seal hunt, the greatest hunt on earth, you understood it was best to name the game for what it was: you copied the leader and leapt from one pan of floating ice to another. When Uncle Gunn rounded the boys up for a game of cockey, as he called it, you knew you were in for a good dare cause he was half cracked and he'd come out with his gaff and you had to run down to the ice with your best stick in hand if you were going to last any time at all out on the ice. Near shore, knowing the water was little more than waist deep, even the youngest boy could coody along over the ice pans at the tail end of the brotherly snake. But when Edgar Gunn led the crowd, there'd always be sharp mothers' voices calling back the young ones, who knew they'd best break from the line and run home at the call of the crow because, if they didn't, the licking they'd get would be something worse than the risk of drowning.

I'll never forget the spring night when I heard the ice breaking up all over the harbour, cracking as though the earth were coming undone at the seams. I knew for sure, because Ron and I spent the night owl-eyed arguing about it, that this was the year I'd be boy enough to join the others who'd be almost-men in the morning, coodying across the harbour with fake gaffs in hand, leaping from pan to pan, proving themselves to be Edgar's copies. Ron said I wasn't ready yet. He said if I was cracked enough to believe I was, then not to expect him to break from the crowd if I tipped a pan and slipped into the water: "Even if you're drowning," he warned. I told him he'd be the one copying me in the morning.

True to spring wind at early morn, Uncle Gunn was down at the landwash herding us into a game. We were nine boys to start, three of them shorter than me. In no time, we were just five in a line caught at the center of the harbour, the littlest ones having bowed out at their mothers' call. As for me, I refused to break from the chain, knowing damn well I'd prove Mum's fussing uncalled for. I was certain I belonged on the ice. I was just one shoe size short of manhood.

We'd come to a big gap. It would take a special leap, if not a sudden spurt in the legs, to get me over it. I was last in line and Ron had just barely cleared what might prove to be a black hole for me. But just because Ron's peter could spit and mine couldn't, that didn't mean I had to give up and give in to Mum's frantic yapping. Ron pointed with his stick from across the black hole and yelled: "Go home before ya falls in, ya fool." But I could see myself as the youngest lad in Bonavista Bay to get his sealing legs. I was gonna jump the black hole, peter spit or no.

I made sure my boots were tied real tight and my coat buttoned all the way. I ran toward the open water and sprang up with arms climbing through the air. As I came down toward the ice I saw my foot fall inches short of the edge, the beginning of the end for sure, because Ron would never let up on the teasing and Mum would sure as hell break my frozen arse with the wooden ladle, but by some tunderin' jesus good luck the ice pan had a lower lip that caught my foot and my left knee landed on the ice. I stepped up with one soaked leg and gave Ron a whack across the chest with my gaff that was no longer a stick. That's when Ron confirmed my life-long suspicion that he was a fool. "Lucky boy," he called me. "Lucky boy!" I said. "Well now, you copy me, my son, if you's so good." I shoved myself ahead in line and held him back with my gaff.

On our way back from the other side of the harbour, Uncle Gunn got us real excited, all savage at the mouth, saying we were taking the path that would lead us to the meanest seal known to Newfoundland: Old Dog Hood. Killing such a monster was no easy job. Only the best of the boys, the truest of the men, would survive the journey, never mind the kill, because Old Dog Hood, he told us, "is the size of a Spanish Bull with more might in one flipper than a whale's got in its tail. And all you've got between you and Old Dog Hood," he said, "is your gaff, so you'd best know how to use it." He started jabbing the gaff into the air, stomping his right foot down with each strike.

There we were, afloat on a big pan of ice in the middle of our tiny harbour, the five remaining boys and Uncle Gunn, two hands on our gaffs, which were no longer straight branches debarked by pocket knives. They were the real tool, the weapon used to survive the greatest hunt on earth. We were madmen ready for war, yelling and stomping and killing the air. The road to Old Dog Hood was a long winding one that took us leaping over every opening in the harbour. We knew Edgar was snaking his way back to the doomsday gap at the center of the cove. Sure enough, before we could drive our gaffs into the beast to prove ourselves boys enough to be called men, we would have to leap the black hole one more time.

My legs were tired and I was shaky at the knees, but I wasn't gonna let the fact that I had now fallen to the back of the line keep me from proving myself. The four other boys made it across. I no longer felt so sure of myself. The gap in the ice seemed bigger, the water darker. I looked homeward. Mum had gone inside. I didn't even have Ron provoking me. I wanted him to yell, "You'll never make it." I needed him to piss me off. He wouldn't do it. He just stood there, looking at me, leaning on his stick, being mean. It was easier to prove myself when I had others to prove wrong. Now I had to prove myself to myself. I knew then that I was still a boy. Mum should not have let me out of the house. I was frozen. Not just cold. Frozen. Filled with fear. Edgar snapped me out of it. "Let's go, Charlie. Ya gotta jump now, cause Old Dog Hood is getting away and I'll be damned if you'll be the one to keep me from killin'im this mornin'." The rest of them, steaming at the mouth, started cheering me on as though I were a miracle child and not some terrified lad lost in rubber boots two sizes too big, trying to see if his mother was at least looking at him from inside the kitchen window when I knew damn well she wasn't. They all cheered, all except Ron. He wasn't even looking my way anymore.

I could have walked around the black hole. I considered doing it. If that had been my choice, I'd have no story to tell, and that's no way to live. In the end, what made me boy enough to be a man on that day is the scar I still got on my arse. Uncle Gunn had to fish me out of the water with his real gaff. He hooked me by the butt cheek and pulled me out from under the ice, where I think I may have been trying to hide. When Mum got her hands on me, I was comforted by her anger. Her fiery voice warmed me as she worked the frozen clothes off my skinny, red body. Some sight to imagine: myself, standing on the kitchen table, bare as a baby lamb with Mum behind me sewing up the new hole in my backside. I had both hands over my peter trying to hide how bald and tiny and frozen it was, terrified that Ron would burst through the kitchen door, pointing at me and laughing. He didn't. After that, all the boys and even Edgar started calling me Lucky Boy. I didn't mind. In fact, I was proud. It was just the right name. Only a fool wouldn't see that.

# If Sister Hadn't

Sister fell through the longers. Can't say how she fell, but down to the water and over the rocks. The stage is taller than Eliol, cause he went under and fetched her up. I was beside sister and then she fell through. Mother says stay off the longers. "Stay away from the flakes," she says, "you's gonna get hurt. It's no place to play." It's because Mikey was there and sister said we needed to get him off. "The flakes is no place for dogs," sister said. We ran out to Mikey and sister got closer, bent low to pick him up. But he ran away. Mikey always runs. Off the flakes. I wanted to follow Mikey and when I reached back for sister, she was gone. The longers can roll, they're big sticks. She soused over into the hole. Eliol carried sister back to the house and now she won't look at me. She won't open her eyes. But I can hear her. She says she can't talk and she can't open her mouth no more. But I hear her. She says it will be like this for a long time. I said I don't want to wait. I want sister again. Mikey tells me he won't run to the flakes no more if sister can come back, if she can wake up. Mother won't let me go talk to sister no more. She says sister's not talking, she's asleep. But I can hear her. Mother says that's good. "Just keep listening," she says. But I need to get into the room. I need to tell sister I'm sorry, but she can't hear me through the door. "Open the door!" Mother won't let me go in. She says the doctor needs to be alone with sister now. "Let me in." I know I hear her. She wants to see me. She needs to talk. I can hear her through the door. "Hey! You Let Me In! Sister says it's not my fault. It's Mikey's fault. He's the one that done it."

# Slut

Spend a full winter in the forest cutting timber, long days so hard on the body your ears hurt, do that just once, and you'll understand this quicker than you can think of your mother's name: the slut that gets me through winter isn't the kettle that boils water for tea at home. All winter my mouth waters for that kettle when all I have is a slut over a fire in the middle of the forest. With work like this, you'd be no different than me. You'd be settling for what you can get.

Just from the thought alone, my chest feels her warmth. Thirsting after her hot tea at lunch keeps me moving the bucksaw until I'm ready to break. Sure, I love the smell of working down the trees, the strong scent that sticks in the nose even when the bush is frozen stiff in the slap of winter. I can work the daylight into darkness, dried salt from the sweat of my brow like chalk over my face when I enter the bunkhouse, buttered in sweat. I smell cleaner than solvent, fresher than bread. But a love for the smell of the forest isn't enough to satisfy a nose like mine.

When I've had enough of the lonely bucksaw job and all I want is to get back home and be near the wife I've loved for what feels like my whole life, I picture my lovely slut with her big handle. Can't blame me. I see her next to the fire with steam rising out her mouth. She pants and whistles, blowing my name into the air like a wish. I'm mad just to be near her and hold my hands over the heat that makes her boil. The smell of her drives me the most, the body that steams out of her mouth.

As I walk towards the fire, finally taking my break to gnaw on a fist of hard tack for lunch with a cup of tea to dip it in, I imagine that she will invite me to sit near her, tenderly holding a cup of her dark tea in my hands. I sit there on a stump and forget the crowd of men around me. Dip the tack and suck the tea. Spend a long winter like that, cutting and hoisting a whole field of spruce, and you'll know what it means to love a slut while longing for your kettle.

# For the Love of Lassie

There was no cow milk on the island, and the goat's milk always made young Stuart think of his grandmother's armpit on a summer's day. There was no honey, either, so how was a lad's craving for the promised land of milk and honey, as was offered to him at church, to be satisfied? For Stuart, it was simple, and he figured it out three days before his eighth birthday, sitting in the pew. The instructions came from a voice deep inside him, one he hadn't heard before: Go hide in the store after Sunday morning service, Stuart. Get yourself an empty can. Pour it half full with Carnation evaporated milk and then pull the plug on the molasses puncheon. Wait for the sweet, black lassie to pour out until you've met your fancy. Stir with your finger. He could never decide if the voice was instinctual or celestial. Either way, he never looked back.

In winter, he froze his fingers waiting for the lassie to come out in a stub that wouldn't even melt inside the milk. But he valued the long, empty time he spent kneeled by the puncheon. It taught him the virtue of patience, and he learned to steady his hand like few people, let alone children, ever do. He saw that life calls for a two-handed grip, which is how he held the cup, every Sunday, ritually, in a secret he never once shared. He'd drink the milk, then chew the lassie ball.

At fifteen, his chest sprouted hair like no one had ever seen. Shortly after marriage, his wife, Charm, nicknamed him Moose Stew. "On account of a thick pelt, of course," she explained, blushingly. By thirty, it was said that from a distance you couldn't tell if Stu had "nar stitch of cloth on his hide." His hair grew "tick as dat," they'd say. Even into his fifties, his head of hair was so full and wiry that Charm could be heard through the window calling him to help her scrub the pots. "Come put your head to work, me love," she'd say.

A man of this sort was rare. He was not tall but sturdy as a brick shithouse—at least that's how men described him. He had all his teeth, which was nothing short of miraculous at the time. His eyes gleamed with youth at an age when bright pupils normally begin to dull. His smarts and nerve had not worn, which he showed by balancing himself on the nose of the widow-maker in a storm, cutting into waves, riding out a dare meant for men half his age. It seemed, as he aged, that Stu had found the fountain of youth. If he had, he wasn't sharing the source with anyone. The women all spoke of it; the men didn't. Everybody wondered, but in all those years nobody thought to follow him as he slipped away shortly after Sunday service and snuck into the store.

The day came when young Charlie, one of Stu's many grandsons, stepped into the store after church with a craving that came from deep within. He needed something sweet, something like the honey mentioned in the sermon. Like his Poppy, he knew that life was to be gripped and, as if by instinct or some other form of command, he reached for what he wanted with both hands, never to let go. He entered the store, fixated as usual on finding what he needed. He thought it strange that Poppy had come here to take a nap. He thought little of the pool of lassie poured out of the puncheon but was interested in the tin cup in Poppy's hand. It was full of dark milk. He drank it and loved it, soiling his collar by pouring a stream of lassie milk down his neck. He put the cup back into his Poppy's hand and stepped away lightly, careful not to wake him. He walked out of the store to begin his long, pleasant journey into the world, leaving a trail of small, sticky footprints behind him.

# Down the Hatch

I don't know what makes the capelin come to shore in such ungodly numbers, but I do know that the cod would eat the capelin clear out of the ocean if it could. And no doubt the seals would do the same to the cod. Cut open a fish or a seal and you'll find a feast in there to feed crowds. The cod eats three times its weight, and the seal is no better— bottomless guts on them. It's as if all they've got to do in life is stuff themselves. Have one great big time. Must be nice. Wish I had half that chance.

For my kind to eat, I need much more than I can handle myself, and that's just to get started. I need a schooner, skiffs, nets, fish-forks, tables, knives, puncheons and puncheon tubs for livers, and nearly half a pound of salt per gutted fish. The provision list runs long as my arm. Flour, salt, sugar, bags of hard tack, barrelled salt beef and pork, dried apricots, raisins, the odd apple, oatmeal, molasses, lard and more lard, and still more than that if I'm gonna feed my crew and cook for months down the Labrador. The tea and tobacco alone could break a back to carry. And all that is just for fetching the fish, all that just to make debt.

We get home after nearly a week of sailing with a summer's catch and go to work with a crowd of women and children unloading the fish from the hold to the wharf to be scrubbed, by mop, in washtubs, carried by handbar and spread over flakes, boughs, and rocks to dry in the sun while we wait maybe a week for it to dry, always ready to yank it all to shelter, fish by drying fish, to keep the lot from going maggoty if the clouds come with rain. They often do.

When all's said and done, the fish properly made and loaded again down the schooner hatch, it's not over yet. And remember, I didn't say a word about how each fish was pulled from the sea in a net to be dumped in the skiff and forked up, still flopping, to deck to table to the splitter and header blades, gutted, split, headed, and tossed down the hatch to the salter to be stacked, soaked in the brine that burns the knees off a man.

All that work and still the pay for fish doesn't just come to me. I have to get the fish to the merchant. So again, each dried fish goes from flake to handbar to wharf to deck, down the hatch to the hold before we sail south three days and see it all come out like a dog's bad breakfast at the foot of the merchant's wharf. And that's where I find what's needed most: a man with a coffer who figures someone needs my fish. In the end, I barely meet my own needs. Some years, I could bust my knuckles at how poorly it all trades off. Months of sailing rigging hauling lifting tugging hoisting bending and breaking your back for a drop in the hat, ol' man. The odd year the scale tips in our favour. I sail home and have one great big time with my crew and my crowd. One day in the year, one year of many, we fill our guts like cod in the capelin or seals in a cloud of cod.

# Last Chance

Eli said what he should never have said. "You's a cowly cat Dorcas." He yelled it out. We were supposed to be picking berries. I tried to ignore him but he stood too quiet, staring down at me as I busied myself with filling Mother's good pot with partridgeberries. He knew that if he said it a second time, the dare would be cancelled out and I could go on picking berries, just as Mother had sent us to do. So I waited, but it was hard. Eli was short but acted tall, casting his shadow over me. He knew what he was doing. I couldn't tolerate my little brother looking down at me, staring at the back of my head, after throwing a dare at my face like a frog down my dress. I had to stand up. I was a head taller.

"No I isn't," I said to his forehead. "Yes you is," he said to my chin. We went on, back and forth, until he added, "Yes you is, Dorcas, and I can prove it." I told him he couldn't. "I'm no cowly cat, Eli, and I can prove it better than you." I woke up that morning knowing this would happen. I knew Eli wouldn't be able to resist the story of the two-headed man that Man had told us the night before. Mother threatened to gut him like a fish, from stomach to throat, if he spoke a word of the old tale to Eli, but when big brother gets started on his stories, it would take an act from Above to stop him. Eli was hooked by the first words: "Never go into the bog for fear of the two-headed man." Eli listened on, eyes shining like licked candy. "The two-headed man rises out of the bog and sneaks up on you. He grabs you by the ankles and turns you upside down so you can't run and you can't fight."

Man knew, as did Mother and I and everybody else, that Eli couldn't leave a good story alone. He had to test it. He had to know if it was true. As we made our way to the berry patch, I knew he had a snake up his sleeve. He knew I didn't back down from dares. We would have to do just like the children in Man's story. "Fine," Eli started, "if you's no cowly cat, go make a mark on the big dead tree in the bog with me, or else you's forever the sissy cowly cat that I knows you is." We left mother's good pot in the berry patch.

We each picked a sharp stone along the path and marched over the hill. We turned into a small, overgrown trail that snakes through the spruce limbs. I was in the lead, Eli's hand fastened to my dress. When I stopped without warning at the edge of the forest, his nose bumped into my shoulder blade. He didn't know what to expect. "Trail ends here, Eli." I hoped his nose would bleed. There was silence. Finally, he spoke, "You took the wrong trail, Dorcas. You's too scared to go into the bog." Saucy little cracky of a child, I thought. "No I isn't," I said. "It ends cause nobody ever goes into the bog." We had reached the spot where all the other children stopped, turned, and ran for home. I hoped Eli had at least one smart crumb in his loaf. He didn't. I decided I needed to move fast, hoping that, once I stretched my foot beyond the edge of the forest and landed it into the bog, he'd flip his heel and run. I grabbed him by the hand and pulled him along, breaking my way through the last limbs.

We could see the empty bog beyond the last spruce branch. There it was, the dead tamarack in the middle, black as night in the orange glow of the late evening sun. I said down to Eli, getting up on the tips of my toes to make him feel small and threatened, "We're not turning back, Eli, we're gonna mark that tree. We're not going home until we mark that tree. Just like in Man's story." He gulped. He said nothing about being afraid. I forged on. "Here we are, Eli. One last step and we're in the bog. This is no time to run." He expected me to push him that way. He saw that I was trying to make him afraid. All I did was spur him into stupidity.

He lashed out. "Well, what are you waiting for? Take it, sissy cat." He hissed *sissy*. "Fine, then, bratty-devil," I said with clenched lips, "but I'm not taking it alone." And, with that, I yanked him to my side, my arm gripped across his shoulders. "Now you remember the dare, Eli. We have to mark the tree. Don't forget what Man said happened to the boy. Once we're in the bog and the two-headed man sees us, he'll get *you* by the ankles. Not me. He'll take *you* first. Boys taste better than girls. Especially saucy ones like you." Eli gulped again. He was hesitating. I was picturing mother's pot left behind in the berry patch. He looked up at me with his big eyes and said, "You's a cowly cat Dorcas!" I shook my head. Brain of a bird in a boy.

We went in together. Lifted our legs out of the forest and into the bog. I was holding him, moving slowly. The smallest flinch in him and I would turn and run, leave him behind, teach him a lesson. But he was determined not to buckle, not to think. We were standing with our feet in cold moss and muck. The silence in the bog was crushing. We stood frozen, scanning the bog. No sight of him. Nothing. No two-headed man. No one-headed man. No no-headed man. No man, no sir, not whatsoever.

I was terrified. Eli was too. But under all that—his trembling knees and white face with sweat beads the size of gulls' eyes—I saw he was a little disheartened. He sighed, sounding nearly sad. We gripped our stones and stepped on, moving in mirror of each other, feeling better shielded that way. We inched toward the dead tamarack. The sinking sun was burning red beyond the bog, crowning the tree with fire. Its limbs spread like black flames. We were holding each other. I was seeing hellfire. We were tiptoeing into it. Eli looked right, I looked left. We stepped steadily forward into a world turned against us. The sinking sun burst and poured red light down the hill into the bog. The tamarack was Death now. The two-headed man was Death's hungry dog. It was all too clear. We were watching the end of the world, our feet sinking in cold mud. A raven crossed the sky and landed high in the tamarack. Man was right, the two-headed man could see us, no matter what, and he knew exactly when to make his entrance. We were halfway to the tree when he did.

"This is your last chance." The words boomed across the sky and echoed like gunfire in a cave. We were paralyzed. The sun sank deeper, shadows swallowing the hill. I feared I had gone deaf. I was underwater. I heard my heartbeat. That was all—a drowned thump. Then the devil blasted out again: "This is your last chance." Eli's hand slipped from mine. He dashed for the tree. I watched him scurry and heard him screaming like a piglet on fire. I stood there, hesitating. Then I ran, and as I ran, I thought, Why the hell is Eli going to the tree? Why the hell aren't I running for home? Why am I following that brazen bugger? I cursed him and ran in his tracks, thinking the while that I ought to leave him to his lesson, let the two heads argue over who bites first. And I thought, if I do that, Mother will say it was all my idea to drop the pot and go into the bog. Meanwhile, he'll be dead without having had to tell Mother the truth, and that's not fair. As Eli leaped up into the tree, I was clawing onto his back.

The world was sunk inside a blood sky. We had dropped our stones. Perched in branches, we each took a long scun for the monster. No sight of him. An empty world. A dead bog. The raven circled. No voice, no more shock, just the wind caught in dead branches. The tamarack creaked and we panted. The hollow bog. And yet it was filled. We saw how the dead live on—why they call down the red sky. The voice, a phantom gale, cut across us again. The echo was metallic as before. "This is your last chance."

This monster was far greater than the one in the story. We kept staring, watching for him to appear out of the mud. But he was nowhere to be seen. I thought, for a moment, maybe the raven is his eyes. He must be seeing us from above. We felt cheated in all this. If nobody really knows what he is, they should never say a word about him. Many had told the story, not only Man, and nobody ever said he was invisible, or that he worked with a raven. They just said he'd sneak up and get you by the ankles. We weren't prepared for this type of torture. Just as I was about to say to Eli that maybe we were hearing some other kind of voice, it was like the two-headed man could read my thoughts. "This is your last chance," he said, "before we come for you."

Now it was a truth. It was a fact of the world. Like gravity. If the monster didn't have two heads, it wouldn't have said "we." It would have said "I." I had learned that much about language in school. I whispered to Eli, "We're gonna have to make a run for it." He nodded, and we hit the soggy ground in full flight. The voice boomed as we ran, saying, "If you don't come out, we will come in for you. This is your last chance. Come out on your own. If you can."

The trickery of stories. Nobody ever said the two-headed man was considerate. I thought maybe we were blessed. Maybe he was giving us a last chance to leave the bog and leave him alone. Maybe he was a generous, misunderstood monster. Such a thing is possible. Stories aren't always fair. We rushed over the field of moss like mice fleeing a hawk. Soon we were out of the bog and into the forest, plowing wildly through spruce limbs, heading for the road home, down the hill and around the harbour into Mother's arms. I felt hopeful for the first time in all this. I started pitying the misunderstood monster of the bog. He never bothered any of us. He never came looking to mark our house with a stone. But that feeling quickly changed.

Before we could break out of the bush and find the path, the voice surrounded us. The red of the closing sky doused the forest. The black limbs reached for our arms and faces like spider legs. The voice threatened, "We will now come for you!" Man's story never prepared us for that. The two-headed man was never said to leave the bog and chase children through trees. We panicked, running wildly, scraping our arms in the branches. We'd lost the path. We could only plow deeper into a web of limbs. I was sure I was hearing the two-headed man, steadily gaining. We were running and running but getting nowhere. I heard him. His breath at my legs. He was reaching for my ankles, his arms low beneath the branches, his claws closing at my feet. I knew I felt him, knew I would be caught. With that, I fell into thin air—the open.

I saw Eli tumble into the clearing of the path. I was still at his side, tumbling with him. We jumped to our feet and looked at each other but didn't bother looking for the monster. We knew he was with us. We made for home in a mad gallop. I could see it wasn't over yet. The voice filled the air again, repeating, "We are now coming after you." It was hardly news. We scurried on. Down the hill toward the water! We knew if we reached the shore, we'd be in open view from across the harbour and the monster would finally give up. We saw the water through the trees and were screaming to big brother Man and Skipper Malcolm, telling them to be ready to fight off the two-headed man. I began to think we were reeling in the monster. We would be heroes.

On a boulder at shore, we stopped dead. We couldn't scream anymore. All that was over. The chase hit a wall. It felt like a storybook slammed shut. We were out of breath, yes, but that isn't why we were speechless. We had no words to say or think. We were staring, mouths agape, at the first iron ship we had ever seen. Enormous. She barely fit inside the harbour. She was all white, with red lettering across her nose. She was like nothing we had ever imagined. The sight of her had choked us.

Until that day, we had only understood smaller boats, had seen only the odd schooner. They were always made of wood, built by hand. The letters across the bow of this one read *Christmas Seals*. When we got home, there was a man in a white coat in the kitchen. He said we had arrived just in time. He said we had to go with him. Mother said it was alright and told us, "Everybody has to go with him."

When we got on deck, another man in a white coat explained something to us about an x-ray. He said something else about tuberculosis and led us into a chamber with a bed and a machine over top of it. I didn't know what he meant or what he was doing when he made me lay down on the hard, metal bed. I laid there with a heavy strap over my eyes. There was music echoing inside the metal walls of the chamber. It sounded unnatural. I had heard it on deck as we were led into that strange room. The music screeched out of speakers attached to the ship's cabin. Everybody's voice fell hard to the steel deck when they spoke. I had never heard of speakers before, or voices hitting sheets of steel. I didn't know how to listen to my heartbeat as I lay on that bed. It sounded dry. I didn't know it could.

If I looked anything like Eli being led into the x-ray chamber—his face was stone grey—the crew might well have thought the photos they were taking would prove we were sick, and they would feel like they were heroes, come in time to save us. I didn't understand what the man in white meant when he said "photos of our insides." I tried to picture it when I went to bed, holding the sheets tight against my throat. I couldn't see it. I felt confused. Mostly, I felt injured. I realized that the story of the two-headed man had come true, but it wasn't at all like brother Man or the others had said it would be. The monster had come for us, true, only he was neither two-headed, nor a man.

# Learning to Take It

We're nearing the end of the hunt and are in real bad need of a good scrub-down from head to toe to kill all the bloody lice. The lot of us stinks enough to make gulls lose their breakfast. But we endure it. Not much of a choice. That's just how swiling is. You live in seal fat and sleep on stacks of greasy pelts. At lunch, we pick maggots out of the hard tack to eat it, but that's not the problem. What burns me is the lice. I could duck my head in a bucket of fire if it meant getting rid of them. They scuttle under the skin, they live in your scalp and make their way into every crevice and hole of your body. They've kept me awake, three nights now. Last night, the old man across from my bunk, Sam Lane from Heart's Content, showed me a trick I never want to use. He gets out of his bunk, pulls off his trousers, takes off his underwear, turns 'em inside out and puts 'em back on. Yanks up the trousers and jumps back into his bunk and sighs, feeling much better about it all. I whispered, "What d'ya do that for Sam?" He says, "Couldn't sleep. Couldn't sleep, b'y, dey tore it out of me so bad. This way I figures I'll be dead to the world before dey tears into me again." That's how you get adjusted, I guess. Turn yourself inside out and hope for the best. It's not right. It's no way to live. I bet Sam's been out here fifty years or more, and look at him. He still can't just roll over and take it. He says he does, but no man sleeps through that. I hope to Christ things are different for me when I'm the old man across the bunk. I hope I won't be hauling off my clothes in the middle of the night. Not as a poor old man. Not for lice.

# On My Knees in the Flowers

Yes, I'm crying. It does make me cry. Not ashamed of it. No sir. You spend fifty-two years, every summer on your knees along the Labrador, and you'll know what it means to see a potato flower. First time I seen this since I was eight year old. First time I get to stand in a spring garden since I was a boy. I remember being in the garden with Mother, that's more than sixty years gone. And yet no farther away than yesterday, that memory of Mother, and the same of sister too. I saw potatoes flower then. Oh, but you forget it. You have to spend your life with your face in fish guts to know what it means. Never mind that, it's not so bad as it could've been. Sure, now I live alone. Audrey's gone, love of my life. But I still keeps her by my side. It's not like you can just let go of someone like her. I know she's dead, I don't need no photo to remind me of that. I know she's gone. But she's still here too. It don't matter if you don't see her. I do, and it's not foolishness either. You can't imagine what she did for me.

She used to cut up her nightgown when it got worn, cut up all that lovely material and sew it into the knees of my long underwear, on the insides of them. I started work as a salter, see. In the hold along with my father since I was nine year old. And the salter is the worst of the jobs. I knows, cause I done 'em all. Header for a long time and splitter too. But more than forty summers I salted, and in the year I first come home to my new, lovely wife, someone finally saw what it was like for me, how bad it was on my knees. See, Mother had passed on when I was nine year old. Tuberculosis took sister too. After that, I had nobody to be tender to me, not 'til I met my Audrey. Father was good, good enough, but not a soft man. Men weren't soft then. And he never married again. Audrey cried, she did. Yes she did, when she saw me the first fall I come home. She could hardly look at how raw and scarred my knees were, cut and beaten. The skin was burned by salt and looked no better than fish meat. Imagine, eighteen hours of the day kneeling on rough wood, your legs soaked in brine like pig's feet. Imagine how that felt. You can't. Blisters and cuts and slivers, all soaking in fish brine, the whole summer long.

The next year, and every year after that, more than thirty of them, she kept my knees safe with her nightgowns. That's what she done, that's the way she was, Audrey was. Little patterns of flowers, soft as pillows, to keep my knees from being torn open. From being burned by the salt. So now you know why little flowers get to me, why they make me cry. Even little potato ones, they make you cry. Not ashamed of it.

# The Fetch

When you're wandering in the fog though you've walked the same path a thousand times since childhood, it can happen that you no longer know where you are. And if ever you lose yourself in this way, walking in the fog along your normal road, there's a good chance you'll come face to face with a figure you'll take to be a stranger. He'll appear like a statue out of thick fog. Then he'll come toward you. "Good evening sir," he'll say to you. "Good evening to you, sir," you'll say right back, whether you mean to or not.

This happened to me one night. I was walking over to Sydney Cove for a game of Five Hundreds with Caleb Brown and some of the b'ys when the fog came on so thick I could have written my name in it. I'm not too sure how I got so lost, but all of a sudden I was standing near the water's edge. I couldn't see water, the fog was that thick, but I could hear it coming into land. This is very odd, I thought. There's no way I could have come all the way to the water without walking flat into the back of Uncle Gar's house. I know my way to Caleb's. I've been walking there every other night since I was no taller than three stacked apples.

But on this night I couldn't make sense of where I was or how I had gotten there. I turned right to follow the shoreline. I clambered over boulders and around trees. I wasn't worried. I knew I'd eventually find my way to Sydney Cove, probably walk right into Gar's house like I should have in the first place. I came around one of the trees and saw what appeared to be a man, barely visible in the fog and dark. He was still as a statue. It made me think I must have fallen into a dream—maybe I was actually at home, snoring away in the rocker. But that couldn't be right. I never miss a game of Five Hundreds. So I figured I must've slipped on a rock along the path and bumped my head. This wasn't right, this statue, not real at all. Then the shape stepped towards me. It moved slow, like it was pushing its way through water and not fog. Then it spoke, sounding all too real: "Good evening, sir." I could scarcely speak back, or even breathe right, my mouth was so dry with fear. I wanted to turn and run, but that wasn't a real option. Instead, my body just stepped towards the stranger and my mouth said, without any other part of myself meaning to, "Good evening to you, sir." Croaked it out.

I could see his face well enough to know this man was no stranger. He was familiar. He looked like a cousin, or even a brother, but yet I knew I didn't know him entirely. I wanted to say his name, but I didn't know that much. "May I walk with you?" he asked. And with that he reached out for my arm and took me by the elbow. I tried to say, "That would be fine, sir," but couldn't get it out. I had no words of my own. I was sure I no longer had lips. I couldn't feel my face. But I was breathing fine. Strangely, I wasn't afraid anymore. I felt quite safe with him. He held me by the arm and guided me through the fog.

He led me through the trees and helped me over the many boulders along the shore, always keeping his hand on me, either on my arm or shoulder or back. Always touching me, never having trouble with his own footing or balance. He didn't say a word more and didn't try to look me in the face either. In fact, whenever I got a clear glimpse of his head, his face was turned away. I started to believe he didn't have a face because I never saw it the whole time he guided me. There were a lot of things I wanted to ask him, thoughts I had in my head that I didn't have words for. It was just like in a dream with things showing up in your head that you never knew could be there. He had me moving along at such a steady pace that even if I had the words I couldn't have talked to him. I needed to watch every step or I'd tumble over and he'd be gone—I don't know how I knew this—and I'd be left behind, lost along that strange shore.

We entered a clearing and were walking easily down the path to Sydney Cove, his arm hooked into mine, his face looking sharply away. I realized I had given up on trying to talk with him, and that's when he spoke: "What's your name," he asked. I tried to say it. Again, as if imprisoned by silence, I couldn't get a word out. But this time, things got worse. I started to panic. I bent my head and tapped my chest as if to check if I was inside my own body. I felt hollow. His question sucked the life out of me. I knew I didn't have a face anymore. I no longer had a name. I could hardly breathe. I had become him. We were men with no faces and no names. And I was sure, in that moment where I saw I was dead, we were one man. I was my own stranger. And just when I was about to forget who and where I was and start turning into something like the fog, the stranger let go of my arm. "Elias Pritchett!" My name jumped out of my mouth like I was sick with it. I took the breath a drowning man would gulp if he found a pocket of air. We had arrived at Caleb's door.

I could see inside Caleb's kitchen through the door window. I could see the clock on the wall above the table. It wasn't quite midnight. It had taken me a long time to get there, more than two hours. It should have taken fifteen minutes. I looked at the stranger and saw the glow of the kitchen lamp shine off his cheek. I saw every one of his features, even the patterns in his eyes. I reached up to touch his face—I had to know if the person I was seeing was real. As my fingers got close to his cheek, he startled me by speaking. "Good Evening to you, sir," he said. I could no longer move my hand towards him. Without intending to do so, I said, "Good Evening, sir," unsure where the words had come from. And with that, he was gone.

Caleb opened the kitchen door and said they started without me. I had just sat down when good Aunt Mary Brown came in from the fog and moonless night. When she spotted me, her jaw dropped. She turned the colour of flour. "What is it, Mary?" Caleb asked. She looked me straight in the eyes, and started to shake. "But I just... How did you..." She didn't have the breath to finish. Caleb caught her as she fainted. I got out of my chair and walked towards her. I kneeled down and took her by the arm. "I don't know," I said, as she came around, "I just don't know."

## Notes and Acknowledgments

I came to this book through my father who was born into a tiny outport called Round Harbour, on Pork Island, an island belonging to the Fair Islands of Bonavista Bay. As is the case with many outport communities, it was resettled in the late 1950s. I could not have written this book without having interviewed a great number of people who had once lived in communities like the one my ancestors founded in the early 1800s. That said, while the island names and description of their placement are true to the geography of Bonavista Bay, all characters are fictional and any resemblance to persons living or dead is coincidental.

While in Newfoundland for research, I was the very fortunate guest of Daisy Rogers (1932-2009), Esther and Stue Rogers, Mabel and Alan Rogers, and Beth and Samuel Gibbons, to whom I am much indebted for having offered me a glimpse into a past I could never have been exposed to through books and museums and archives alone. I especially thank Stue and Esther for the use of their cabin in Round Harbour where I stayed among ruins, listening and trying to learn a thing or two about a world long gone. Thanks also to Claude Rogers in St. John's.

"Last Chance" rightfully belongs to Mabel Rogers, who lived it for real and tells it best. I thank her for having allowed me the honour of interpreting it. "On My Knees in the Flowers" was inspired by a personal account that Skipper Albert Morgan of Glovertown shared with me about his own life as a Labrador fisherman. I am grateful to Skipper Morgan for the long hours he shared with me. With the exception of those mentioned above, these stories are imagined ones with much of their details drawn from research I did at Memorial University of Newfoundland's Folklore and Language Archives (MUNFLA) and from interviews with community elders of the Bonavista Bay region. *The Dictionary of Newfoundland English* was vital to my writing and may be helpful to readers.

I thank the many people who helped me along the way: Stan Dragland, my editor at Brick—this work would have remained in constant want if not for his generous contribution; Warren Cariou, my creative thesis advisor at the University of Manitoba and early guide toward a first book; the good people at the Banff Centre—Greg Hollingshead, Edna Alford, and Don McKay (I thank Don for having known the title when I didn't); Marlene Creates for her encouragement and careful editing; Alayna Munce for the final touches.

I thank the following people and institutions for granting me permission to publish their photographs: Stuart and Esther Rogers (16, 71, 95), Alan and Mabel Rogers (cover, 78, 80), Albert Morgan (35, 62, 83), Clyde Burt (111), The Centre for Newfoundland Studies (12), The Rooms Corporation of Newfoundland and Labrador (68, 76, 90, 92, 115), RedIslandNF.com (22, 24, 28, 32, 42, 45, 50, 88, 108), Newfoundland's Grand Banks Genealogy Site (60, 98), The Sir William F. Coaker Heritage Foundation (55), the Lung Association of Canada (106). Thorough attempts were made to identify the source of the photograph on page 66; my thanks and apologies to the keepers of this image.

The cover photo was taken along the Labrador coast, most likely from the deck of the *Ruby L. Ploughman*, a schooner sailed along the Labrador coast by my great-grandfather, Skipper Roy (1877-1939), my grandfather, Mark Anuel Rogers (1902-1985), and a crowd of cousins and uncles from Round Harbour, Sydney Cove, and elsewhere in the Fair Islands. The photographed schooner was named *Ornate*, but everyone called her the Hornet. She was owned and sailed by Ron and Les Rogers (1921-2005) of Fair Island, Bonavista Bay. I found it a real honour to interview both of these gentlemen. They represent the last of their kind—the Labrador fishermen. When I told Skipper Les I'd be back with more questions, he said, "My son, I don't expect to be around." He was right. He died only a few days after we spoke.

I have written *The Fetch* as an offering to a heritage I have only ever known through stories. This book happened because of my father's love and support. I hear his voice all through these stories, and I cherish that. A closing thank you to Hélène Fournier for having helped grow these stories and for having walked alongside them with me.

**Nico Rogers** is a storyteller and performance artist, and has appeared at writing and folk festivals across the country, as well as on TV and radio. He has taught writing and literature in post-secondary institutions in Ottawa, Winnipeg, and Edmonton and now lives in Toronto, where he is working on a novel which will be a thematic companion to *The Fetch*.